Catch the Wave—
Go Net-Surfing!

The Internet is an awesome new method of communication, a little piece of the future right here and now. Using your own home computer and a telephone line, it's now possible to:

➡ send a message anywhere in the world—in an instant

➡ get your hands on thousands of free computer programs, including demos of the hottest new games

➡ cruise for information through the immense World Wide Web: call a movie studio to see some new trailers, visit your favorite band and download their brand-new video, drop in on a school in a different country, and much more

➡ discuss your favorite music, sports, TV shows, or pets with enthusiasts from all over the world

So get ready to sail the data streams. You're about to surf the Internet—and you don't even need to be online to enjoy the trip!

YOU CAN

SURF

THE NET!

MARC GASCOIGNE

PUFFIN BOOKS

*The author would like to thank Mike Brunton, Demon UK,
Pete Knifton, Sharyn November, Gabe Schuyler,
Richard Scrivener, James Wallis, and the nameless
multitudes online, for all their help and encouragement.
Diamonds.*

PUFFIN BOOKS
Published by the Penguin Group
Penguin Books USA Inc., 375 Hudson Street,
New York, New York 10014, U.S.A.
Penguin Books Ltd, 27 Wrights Lane, London W8 5TZ, England
Penguin Books Australia Ltd, Ringwood, Victoria, Australia
Penguin Books Canada Ltd, 10 Alcorn Avenue,
Toronto, Ontario, Canada M4V 3B2
Penguin Books (N.Z.) Ltd, 182-190 Wairau Road, Auckland 10, New Zealand
Penguin Books Ltd, Registered Offices: Harmondsworth, Middlesex, England

First published in Great Britain in Puffin Books, 1995
First published in the United States of America in Puffin Books, 1996

1 3 5 7 9 10 8 6 4 2

Printed in the United States of America

LIBRARY OF CONGRESS CATALOGING-IN-PUBLICATION DATA
Gascoigne, Marc.
You can surf the net / Marc Gascoigne.
p. cm.
Includes index.
Summary: Describes how the Internet began,
how to get online, and what to do there.
ISBN 0-14-038265-8 (pbk.)
1. Internet (Computer network)—Juvenile literature.
[1. Internet (Computer network).]   I. Title.
TK5105.875.I57G373 1996 004.6'7—dc20 96-20754 CIP AC

Reprinted by arrangement with Viking Penguin, a division of
Penguin Books USA Inc.

THE INTERNET

GETTING ONLINE

EXPLORING THE NET

THE INTERNET

WELCOME TO THE FUTURE

Take a look around. It's almost the year 2000. For decades, scientists and science fiction writers have been trying to figure out what will happen in the future. Unfortunately, most of these predictions have been about personal helicopters, amazing pills that replace food, and sarcastic house-cleaning robots. Not very useful.

But one prediction has come true—in a big way. They said that everybody would be linked to everybody else, via a small computer. The name of this little piece of the future is the Internet, and it's happening right now.

The Internet is an amazing development in computers and communication. It's a cheap and fast way of linking millions of personal computers (PCs) together using normal telephone lines, so people can send messages at incredible speeds. Modern machines can store vast amounts of data, all accessible from your very own PC. Also, because everything is linked together, you can hop from place to place and country to country just by clicking your mouse. You know that big world out there? It just got a lot smaller!

The Internet is a whole new world, just like the ocean or outer space. But unlike the ocean or space, you can explore it yourself—without ever leaving home!

SO WHAT *IS* THE INTERNET, ANYWAY?

Everybody's talking about it, but what does *Internet* actually mean? Literally, the word is short for *inter*-connected *net*-work, and it's a vast spiderweb of computers that are all linked together.

Consider your telephone. From your house, a line runs to the phone company, where it joins all the other local lines. Your local exchange is linked to other exchanges. When you call someone long distance, your signal hops from exchange to exchange, until it gets to the other person's local exchange. From there, the signal is sent to their phone, making it ring. When they answer, the line is opened and you can speak.

Now imagine that your phone line is connected to your home computer—and that you can receive or send stuff from your PC to another computer at the other end of the phone line. It's as simple as that.

In addition to basic messages (known as e-mail), you can send every type of file. That means your PC can send or receive games, programs, pictures, text, sound files, and video clips. You can also use e-mail to join mailing lists and discussion groups where people from all over the globe gather to exchange information on serious and trivial topics.

You know how you can call pre-recorded information lines for the latest sports scores, music charts, and weather reports? It's the same on the Internet. Using your PC, you can access several million sites, devoted to every subject you can think of—and many more you can't! These provide pictures as well as sound, and can also hold music and video files that can be played back on your PC.

And all of these "surfing" references?

These places are all joined together by a set of connections called the World Wide Web. When you look up information in a reference book, you might be sent to another page for more details about a topic. The Web

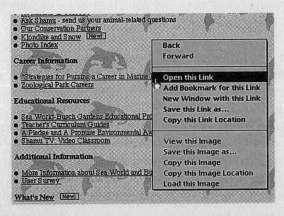

works like that too, but instead of all that page-turning, you just point your mouse and click—and you're at the new place! Moving from site to site like this is called *surfing*.

F Y I

This means For Your Information. In these boxes you'll find snippets of useful or trivial information. Here's the first one: new Internet users are called *newbies*. You might think that all those grizzled old hackers who surf the Net wouldn't like newbies, but in fact there are hundreds of neat sites specifically designed to help newcomers get started.

What's the difference between . . .

You might hear the Internet being referred to as cyberspace, or the World Wide Web. They aren't the same thing.

Cyberspace, a term invented by science fiction writer William Gibson, means the entire electronic world in which the Internet works. It's the abstract electronic space between your telephone or computer and everyone else's.

The *Internet* (or just the *Net*) is the worldwide network of computers that occupies most of cyberspace. Using its millions of connections, people can send and receive letters, files, and information from all over the world.

The *World Wide Web* is the largest part of the Internet, the place where all the new developments are happening. The Web is the interactive, information-browsing area, with each amazing location linked together so you can move from one to the next in an instant.

Who uses the Internet?

Only computer geeks in thick glasses with pocket protectors use this Internet thing, right?

Wrong! Because the Internet is now pretty easy to use, you'll find people from all walks of life: rock stars, writers, teachers, athletes, kids, grannies, doctors, slackers, politicians and businesspeople. There are famous people and everyday folk, young and old, moms and dads, boys and girls.

And more are joining every single day. There are now more people with access to the Internet than live in a medium-sized country—50 million and growing! With the Net growing by more than 10 percent every month, there are an awful lot of people out there.

Who controls the Internet?

Bluntly, nobody. Because the Net is made up of small exchanges linked together, nobody is in charge of anything larger than their own little corner. And because every little section relies on its links with all the other sections to support it, everyone has to cooperate. As a result, the Internet has developed as a free, open-minded world where everyone can be themselves. Yes, there are some people who misuse this newfound freedom, but the vast majority of Net users are responsible.

F Y I

If you do something really annoying on the Internet, you might get *flamed*. That means that people will fill your electronic mailbox with angry messages telling you what they think of you. Don't worry—you have to really mess up to get flamed. People have been flamed for e-mailing junk mail and ads (that's called *spamming*), and for being obnoxious in discussion groups.

Of course there are rules, just like in real life. If you are rude or disruptive, people will tell you what they think of you. If you break the law, you'll have to face the police, like in the outside world. That's just common sense. But beyond that, there are no big scary corporations telling you what you can or can't do on the Net.

Because of this, some areas of the Net are intended for adult audiences only. Just as young people can't, for example, buy alcohol, modern Net software often includes protection programs that can stop kids accessing stuff meant for adults.

A BRIEF HISTORY LESSON

The Internet didn't leap into existence overnight, although it might seem that way. It has grown over the past twenty-five years, and now is large and sophisticated enough for normal, nonscientist types to be able to use it easily. From now on, it's going to expand at an incredible rate, until it's linked the whole world.

HOW IT ALL BEGAN

Back in the late 1960s, the U.S. government was worried about what would happen to communication lines if there was a nuclear war. So military authorities created a network of computer links between all the various defense departments, through which they all shared information. The idea was that if one section was destroyed by a bomb, the connections could go down another path. This network was called ARPANET, and it joined together just 37 computers—though back

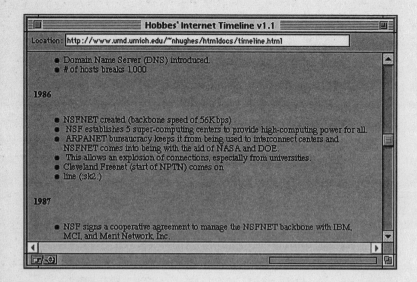

then, of course, computers were massive machines that filled whole rooms.

Thankfully for us, there never has been a nuclear war. The network, however, grew and grew, as universities and other parts of the U.S. educational system joined it to exchange and access data. Because the professors often knew more about computers than the generals, they began calling the shots. As a result, in 1983, a separate network called MILNET had to be established for the military. The places where the two networks joined were called *gateways*, the invention of which would be very important to the future Internet.

NSFNET

The next major U.S. network was NSFNET. It was created in 1984, by another department of the government, the National Science Foundation (hence the name). The department had five computer centers where scholars could use the latest, fastest machines.

NSFNET's goal was to set up a network so people all across North America could access these computers—so it built one, connecting it to ARPANET through more gateways. Soon thousands of schools and universities were joining the new network.

In fact, by 1987 NSFNET was so overloaded with users that it had to be overhauled. It was reopened with much faster connections and computers, and because of a new system it could be available to anyone who wanted to join—even in different countries. Similar networks in all these other countries began to connect to NSFNET using the gateway system, creating an ever-expanding computer world. A few companies were formed to sell such connections.

Over the last eight years, the home computer explosion has allowed many people with powerful PCs to use this network too. A way to make the Internet easy to use for everyone was needed.

CERN invents the Web

The computers accessing the networks were using text-only programs that were clunky and unreliable, and you needed a brain like Albert Einstein's to operate them. That is, until the advent of the World Wide Web.

The Web is incredible. Now you don't need to learn lines and lines of code. Instead of bare text in tiny computer type, information sites on the Web come up as "pages," with pictures, logos, properly laid-out headings and paragraphs, and music and video clips.

The World Wide Web was developed in Switzerland in the early 1990s, at the European Laboratory for Particle Research (known as CERN for short, from its name in French). The scientists there wanted to simplify the way researchers could access all the data they required. The answer was *HyperText Mark-Up Language* (HTML).

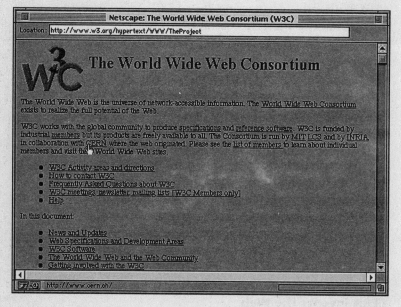

HTML allows documents to include *hyperlinks*. This means that certain key words or pictures can be linked to a related file somewhere else on the network. Now you just click on a word and you are taken instantly to where it is explained or expanded upon. The Web is simply amazing and amazingly simple to use. It's no wonder that it's the fastest growing and most popular area of the Internet.

WHAT'S NEXT?

There are already twice as many people using the Internet as the entire population of Australia, with thousands more joining every week. The United States is the most online country in the world, because this is where the Internet revolution started, but most Western countries are catching up fast. Other nations are also seeing the benefits of online communication. By the turn of the century, most homes in developed countries will have Internet access.

The nature of the Net itself is changing. As computers become more powerful, they can handle more animation and sounds than ever before, and as a result Web pages are becoming even more sophisticated. Already there are experiments going on with 3-D icons; instead of being a name and a line of text, each person in an area like a newsgroup can be represented as a computer-generated animated figure!

Eventually, the science fiction dream of an explorable, fully 3-D, virtual reality cyberspace will come into being, and everyday life will literally take on a new dimension. For example, those trips to see Grandma will be a snap—you'll just send your computer-generated self to visit her PC!

How do I get online?

You don't need to have your own PC to enjoy the best of the Internet. The easiest way to get online is to use someone else's access. For young people, this usually means their school. Many schools are aware of the attractions of the Internet and are getting online connections for their students. Eventually every school and college will be on the Net.

Or find a friend who is already online. He or she will be able to give you a guided tour of what's out there and how easy it is to understand.

You can visit a cybercafe: these are relaxed places

where, for an hourly fee, you can explore the Internet. If there's one near you, grab a few pals, forget the Big Mac and fries for once, and go check it out. The staff will be happy to show a newbie like you what to do.

Most public libraries are now renting out Internet access, too. There are even wired laundromats, where you can cruise the Net while your socks are drying!

You could even get online yourself.

Making a connection

All Internet connections work like this:

A *home computer* is bought by somebody (or somebody's cool parents). They pretend it's for doing homework, but really it's more fun to play Doom. They hear about this awesome Internet thing, and decide to get online. So they get . . .

A *modem*, a small box of circuits that's the link between a computer and the telephone line. With the Internet explosion, modems have dropped in price and become quite affordable. One line from the modem plugs into the PC, and the other connects to . . .

A *telephone line*. Using some simple communications software, our Nethead can now make a connection between the PC and the local Internet company's Point of Presence (the specific link to the Net). It costs the same as a local phone call. The company gives them . . .

Some *Internet software*. When the Net was forming, the software was weird and hard to use, but nowadays there are many simple programs. If you can figure out a word processor, you can use Internet software!

FYI

People think that all of those hours on the telephone must be really expensive. But if you've chosen your connection wisely, you're only paying for the link between you and your nearest exchange when you're online—so it's only a local call.

WHAT CAN YOU DO ON THE NET?

E-MAIL

Now we come to the bottom line—what people actually use the Internet for. We'll start with the most widely used feature: *E-mail*.

E-mail is short for *Electronic Mail*. It is a method of sending messages directly from computer to computer and it's seriously fast. Just imagine: a friend on the other side of the world can get your letter a minute after you write it!

In many ways e-mail is like using the regular postal service. To send someone e-mail, you write a letter on your computer. Then you use a program to send the message over the Internet to your friend's PC. There it is received by a similar program and stored in the computer equivalent of a mailbox (so it doesn't matter if the person is there or not). The next time they check their mail, your letter can be called up for them to read.

E-mail saves you more money the farther away the other person is. Because you're only making a local phone call, you can e-mail someone in Japan as cheaply as if they lived on the next block. Since it's so speedy and convenient, e-mail is incredibly popular, with many hundreds of thousands of messages being swapped every day.

And e-mail isn't just for sending letters to your friends. Keep an eye out for the e-mail addresses of famous people, companies, and television shows. Many sites on the World Wide Web also include an e-mail address so you can send in your comments.

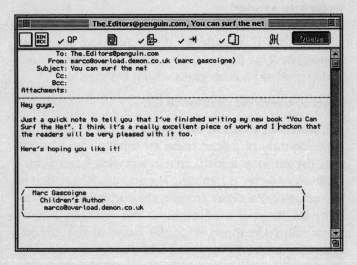

Sending other things

Using e-mail, you can send people homework assignments, articles, pictures, and computer programs. Of course, such items will have to be in a form that a computer can handle. E-mail programs allow you to link all kinds of computer files and send them together.

For example, your best friend could get an e-mail that says: "Hey, have you played Ninja Bunny Wars yet? It's totally awesome! Check it out!" Just imagine the look on your friend's face when the game is right there with your message, ready for him or her to play!

Return to sender

Everyone connected to the Internet has an e-mail address that is specific to them, just like a regular house, street, and city address. Here is a typical e-mail address; see if you can guess who it belongs to:

marco@overload.demon.co.uk

You read it in sections, backwards from right to left. *uk* is the country of origin; these are usually very obvious (yes, the author is British). *co* tells you what type of organization or server is handling the address. Before that is the name of the *service provider*, the particular firm handling the Internet connection; in this example, a company called Demon. Last is the name of the person, company or specific computer with the connection. The @ marks the end of the address itself. On the other side of the @ is the name of the actual person who sent the e-mail; many different people can share one address, each with his or her own electronic mailbox.

If you don't know someone's e-mail address, there are several programs that can help you find it. Failing that, you could always call and ask them!

Types of organizations

com	International company	mil	Military
		net	Internet-related
edu	School, college, or university	org	Other, nonprofit organization
gov	Government		

Country codes

See where your e-mail has come from:

aq	Antarctica	it	Italy
au	Australia	jp	Japan
at	Austria	mx	Mexico
be	Belgium	nl	Netherlands
ca	Canada	no	Norway
ch	Switzerland	nz	New Zealand
de	Germany	pl	Poland
dk	Denmark	pt	Portugal
es	Spain	sw	Sweden
fi	Finland	tr	Turkey
fr	France	tw	Taiwan
gr	Greece	uk	United Kingdom
ie	Ireland	za	South Africa
in	India		

FYI

E-mail addresses in the United States don't include a country code. In the old days, only American computers were connected to the network, so they didn't need a country code to identify them. It's like British stamps not featuring a country name because the British invented the postal service.

Mailing lists

Mailing lists are discussion groups that send out messages to everyone who asks to be included. There are mailing lists for just about every subject under the sun—from nuclear physics to Magic trading cards to German shepherds. You simply e-mail the mailing list's electronic address and ask to join. From then on, every message posted to that address by a member of the list is sent out to everyone else, including you. It's like subscribing to a daily newspaper—but it's free. The most popular mailing list administrating program is called Listserv, and as a result mailing lists are often also known as *listservs*.

Be warned: some mailing lists are very active and can take up a lot of space on your computer. Some can be boring, so once the initial excitement of receiving tons of messages has worn off, only join lists on subjects that you are really interested in!

Smileys

When you are writing a long e-mail message, some of the things you want to say can be very long-winded or hard to express. Happily, there are shortcuts. One is *smileys*, symbols that stand for commonly used sayings or emotions. They're made using simple punctuation; turn them sideways to read them. Most people only use the first two, but, well, things have gotten out of hand!

Regular happy	:-)	Batman	B-)
Regular sad/frown	:-(	Beard	:-)>
Angel	O:-)	Big nose	:+)
Angry	:-||	Black eye	?-)
Annoyed	:-t	Bow tie	:-)X
Asleep	|-)	Broken glasses	R-)
Bald	(:-)	Broken nose	:^)

Burp	:-*	Laughing out loud	:-D
Bushy eyebrows	I:-)	Licking lips	:-9
Cow	3:-)	Monkey	:- I
Cross-eyed	%-)	Ouch!	:-()
Crying	:'-(	Pig	:8)
Crying buckets	:'''-(	Punk with	
Devil	} :>	mohawk	=3D:-)
Disappointed	:-e	Puzzled	:-?
Distracted	%^)	Robocop	I-]
Drooling	:-L~~	Screaming	:-@
Duck	{:V	Shocked	:-O
Dunce	<:-)	Shouting	:-V
Elvis	5:-)	Silent	:-X
Evil grin	>:-)	Sour taste	
Flamed	~~:-(	in mouth	:-6
Foot in mouth	:-!	Speaking	:-v
Frenchman		Teeth in braces	:-(#)
in beret	/:-)	Tired (yawning)	I-O
Frog	8)	Tongue-tied	:-&
Glasses wearer	8-)	Undecided	:-/
Got a cold	:-'	Vampire	:-[
Headphones	[:-)	Wearing baseball	
Hmmm		cap	d:-)
(bemused)	:-}	Winking	;-)
Jaw drops on floor	:-C		

Smileys are also called *emoticons*, a combination of "emotion" and "icon." When you send e-mail, only use smileys when they are needed; don't stick hundreds in unless you are having a bad day. And don't ever use them in your homework unless you want to stay in school for the rest of your life.

NEWSGROUPS ON THE USENET

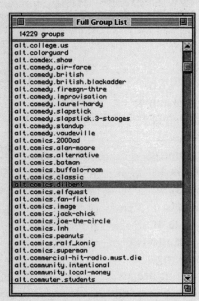

Sending e-mail to your friends—or dashing off vital comments to the president about his foreign policy or to a Smashing Pumpkins fan club about the band's latest video—is all pretty great. But computers can do far more than that. Instead of just contacting one person, why not get connected to lots of people at the same time? When you drop into a newsgroup on a particular subject, your comments and messages are placed in a public area for all to read—and you can read everyone else's contributions too.

News from the BBS

In the early days of the Internet, users would exchange news or gossip by dialing into their local *BBS*, or Bulletin Board System. However, the quality of the information was hampered by the BBSs being separate from each other, relying solely on their own users for information.

Nowadays, with the Internet connecting every corner of the globe, BBSs have for the most part been replaced by a linked series of bulletin boards, or *newsgroups* as they are now called. The area of the Internet where all the newsgroups reside is called the *USENET*, originally created by two American university students, Jim Ellis and Tom Truscott. It's an enormous series of discussion groups, where more than *thirty thousand* messages get posted on an average day. If a mailing list is like having a newspaper delivered to your house, joining a newsgroup is like going to the store to buy one.

Users using USENET

There are now more than fourteen thousand different newsgroups. Why so many? Because each newsgroup covers only one subject. If you want to talk about another topic, you have to switch to the relevant newsgroup.

These subjects might be general, such as "sports" or "computer games."

> **FYI**
>
> Joining a newsgroup is called *subscribing*, but this doesn't mean you have to send any money to anybody. The only thing newsgroups cost is time and space on your hard drive.

They might be very specific, such as "X-Men comics" or "Washington Redskins." A lot of them are really trivial: just check out a newsgroup like **alt.swedish.chef. bork.bork.bork** for some Muppet mayhem. Others allow people to discuss important topics with experts like scientists and politicians. The only trouble with using USENET is finding the particular newsgroup you want.

Everything in moderation

Some newsgroups are moderated, which means that all of the postings are read by the person in charge of the group. The useless ones are trashed and only the pertinent comments or questions make it onscreen. Being a moderator is quite a job, and some groups are updated much less often than unmoderated ones—although the quality of the discussion is usually better.

USENET subject codes

If you're checking out the USENET, it's important to get some clue as to what type of newsgroup you're looking for. Every group is put in a particular category with similar ones, and all of them have a descriptive name. Some of the groups are very obscure, especially those about technical computer stuff; only programmers and other geeky types will need them. The most common ones are listed here:

alt.	Alternative and trivial stuff	news.	News about USENET and newsgroups
biz.	Business matters		
comp.	Computers	rec.	Recreation, entertainment, hobbies
k12.	Education from kindergarten through twelfth grade	sci.	Science and research
misc.	Anything that doesn't fit anywhere else	soc.	Social science, psychology, etc.
		talk.	Debate on topical subjects

There are also newsgroup categories for different states and cities (e.g., ba. for Bay Area, San Francisco or cle. serving Cleveland, Ohio) and many countries (from aus. Australia to za. South Africa). Some universities and colleges have them (e.g. nyu. New York University). Different Internet service providers may also provide their own newsgroups to relay information about their service (e.g. aol. America Online). A new category is up-to-the-minute newsfeeds, such as clarinet.; these cost money, and are generally used by big businesses.

What's the news?

To access a newsgroup, you need a simple program called a *newsreader*. It tracks down the newsgroup

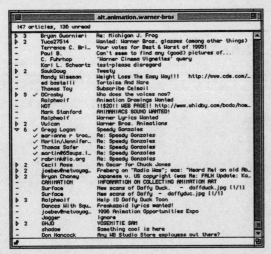

you want, helps you read whatever's been posted there, and allows you to add your own comments to the debate.

Different parts of a discussion are called *threads*. The newsreader program keeps each particular set of threads together so you can follow the argument as it develops.

Newsgroups don't stop when you are offline. Once

FYI

When you first join a newsgroup, you should always read the accompanying *FAQ* (Frequently Asked Questions) file, if there is one. It'll probably answer three-quarters of your queries immediately! Then lurk for a while, reading the postings to see what's going on, before you send any comments of your own.

you've subscribed to them, USENET will continue storing everyone's messages. Every time you turn on your newsreader, the recent additions to the discussion will be waiting for you to read.

FILE TRANSFER

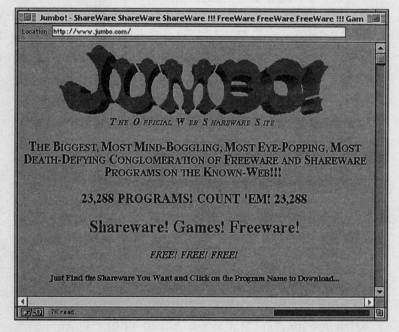

This section should really be called Free Stuff! *File transfer* is simply a more sophisticated version of e-mail. Using a very simple program (like CuteFTP or Fetch), you can call up one of over forty thousand data banks throughout the world and download as much free software as your hard drive can hold!

When you join the Internet, the company making the connection for you (your service provider) will give you all the software you need to send e-mail, download programs, and explore the World Wide Web. After that, you'll find that the best way to get more software is to use file transfer and get it off the Internet itself!

Of course, you will also find literally thousands of other types of programs, whatever your type of computer. There are games, fonts, applications, graphics, and sound programs; you name it and it's bound to be available. Game companies use the Net for advertising and promotion; they post demo versions of their hottest new releases as downloadable files so you can try them out before spending your hard-earned dollars. Software manufacturers sometimes post revised and updated versions of their programs for users to download for free.

Most of the programs are *shareware* or *freeware*, invented by enthusiasts rather than commercial companies. With shareware, if you like the program so much you are still using it after thirty days, you are on your honor to send the small fee noted in the program. Freeware is better, since it doesn't require any payment. There are other types, such as *postcardware*, which asks that you send a postcard showing your home town if you like the program. Best of all is *happyware*: if you like the program, you must grin like an idiot all day long!

FTP it!

File transfer is usually referred to by the short acronym *FTP*. This stands for File Transfer Protocol, the simple code that allows a Net surfer to download a program from a data bank. Some FTP sites are run by firms or educational establishments solely for their members or students, and users need a password before they can access them. *Anonymous FTP* is a type of FTP where you don't need to identify yourself when you log on to the data bank; most FTP sites are like this, and anyone can use them, including you.

Of course, some programs and other files can be very large, and require a long time to transfer to your computer. Most files will be compressed to make them smaller, so you'll need a program like StuffIt Expander or Unzip to expand them; make sure you check out how large a file is before you start downloading. And, though it may seem obvious, it's worth mentioning: programs intended for other makes of computer won't work on yours, even if you can download them. Always double-check to make sure.

IRC ON THE NET

IRC stands for Internet Relay Chat, but everyone uses the initials. It's a real time version of e-mail, where you can have a conversation by sending brief messages back and forth.

There are more than 150 IRC sites; most Internet companies provide access to one or more. Some people have compared IRC to an Internet version of CB radio, and in many ways that's true. Just like CB, an IRC chat takes place on a specific channel, where any interested person can join in; if you want to have a more private chat, there are plenty of side channels to go to.

IRC has recently come into its own as a serious method of communication. During the Gulf War, computer users in Iraq sent out reports of the bombing raids that, unlike CNN's reports, weren't censored by the U.S. military—history as it happened! When rebel

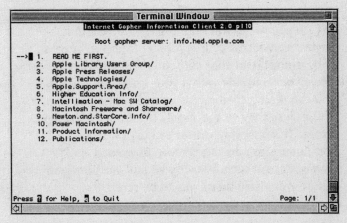

soldiers tried to overthrow the Russian government in 1993, on-the-spot reports were flashed all around the world using IRC! Still, most people use IRC for a light-hearted chat with like-minded folk.

TURN ON THE TELNET

Before the Web was constructed, Internet users were able to access data banks using *Telnet*, a simplified version of what Web users now use as a matter of course. There are still some dusty corners of the Net that you need a Telnet program to explore. Most up-to-date Internet programs have Telnet capability.

Once you're connected, you can use the host computer from your own keyboard, just as if you were right in front of it! This can be fun, but all of your commands will have to be transmitted in simple, non-graphical format. There are no flashing colored icons and downloadable video pictures on Telnet. It's most useful for accessing academic research libraries across the U.S., or the vast data banks of NASA.

FYI

In case you were worrying, there is no way that anyone can access your computer from the Internet. They cannot read your computer files and they cannot infect your machine with a virus from a distance. If you can read something on someone else's computer, it's because they've specifically left it out for everyone to see. The only way viruses can get onto your computer is as part of a file you download via FTP: so *always* scan such files with an anti-virus program before you install them, just to be sure.

THE WORLD WIDE WEB

This is the most amazing part of the entire Net, the home to all that's most useful on the Internet—and all that's totally crazy, too! As the Net expands, the World Wide Web is the star attraction that's persuading ordinary people to get online.

Imagine being let loose in the biggest bookstore or library on Earth. At one end there are encyclopedias, atlases, and reference books of all kinds. Somewhere in the middle are the less serious items: books about movie stars, music, sports, and hobbies. And all the way in the back, where the staff have tried to hide them but failed, there's the hilarious and the strange: the joke books, the games, the collections of nonsense!

The Web is more than just a book library, though: it has video and audio, too. For example, if you're reading about the new Brad Pitt movie, you can click on a

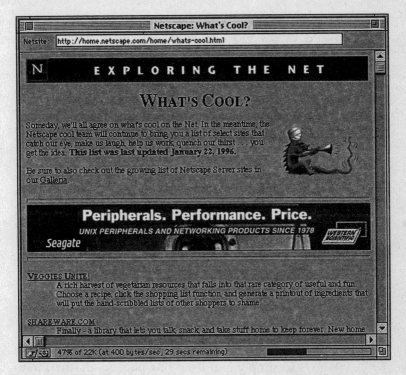

button and download a preview clip! The only limit on the Web is the creativity of the people who design the sites.

On the page

World Wide Web sites are often called pages. When you access them with a program that can show their **graphics**, they come up on your **PC** like the page of a **magazine** or book. Once you've finished, you can call up another site—or jump to another page by clicking on one of the **hyperlinks**.

How do they work? Check out the last paragraph. See the four underlined words? If this was a Web page and you wanted to know what a "hyperlink" was, you'd simply move your mouse cursor to that high-lighted word. Click!

. . . Suddenly, the first page is replaced by another one, which explains that hyperlinks are connections between pages. You make the link work by clicking on it; this tells the program to take you where the link ends.

Not all links are obvious, which is part of the fun. That first paragraph is about Web pages. But if you clicked on "PC," you might find yourself at IBM's online computer showroom. You could have clicked on "magazine" and zapped off to the home pages of your favorite computer monthly. Clicking on "graph-ics" might take you anywhere from a collection of 3-D stereograms to instructions on creating your own Web page.

Surfin' safari

Because of the hyperlinks, the fun way to explore the Web is to simply hop from one page to another, wan-dering here and there at the whim of the links. Every newbie in the history of the Internet has spent his or her first two hours on the Web doing that.

If you need to do some serious research, the hyper-links can really help. Any time you come across a term you don't understand, there'll usually be a link to a definition. Even better, there are connections to simi-lar sites that may look at the topic from another angle, or provide more information. If you're doing a school essay on recycling, for example, it's easy to jump around and see how they recycle in Canada, Germany, outer space, Cleveland . . . Using the Web might even get you psyched about doing your homework!

Who weaves the Web?

So who sticks all this great stuff up—and why? Some sites are, to a greater or lesser degree, advertisements. Compare them to TV "infomercials" or newspaper "advertorials" (advertisements in a newspaper or a magazine that are disguised as articles). This doesn't matter when the pages are a selection of Warner Brothers or Sub Pop's current hot bands, complete with video clips, sound files, and discographies. These sites

may run for many hundreds of pages, crammed with graphics and links to thousands of others.

Many more pages are run by real fans. That's why so many Web pages seem to be about music, movies, TV, sports, or hobbies. These people are enthusiasts of the right kind, people who want to talk about their own favorite interest, and share their knowledge. Their sites are usually upbeat and informative, and among the most creative, too.

Some people are obsessed only with themselves, or with dull subjects, and it's their Web pages you have to watch out for. There are more than enough great sites around, so don't worry when you hit a dud. Just keep surfing—there's another incredible Web page at the end of that next link!

FYI

As you'll read in the World Wide Web directory at the end of this book, there are some spectacularly useless Web pages. You want a page written totally in Klingon? You can't live without an in-depth discussion of bath sponges or sock puppets? You really need to see a Pop Tart explode? The Net has them all. Aren't you lucky?

GETTING ONLINE

Whether you have your own PC or only get fifteen minutes a week fighting the twenty other Netheads in your class, you'll need to know how to get around the Internet. The very best way to learn anything new is to have someone teach you face-to-face. If you have access through school or via a friend, this will be no problem. Similarly, if you visit a cybercafe, the staff will be happy to show you the basics, and certainly enough to get you started.

To be able to take full advantage of all the Net has to offer, though, you'll need to know how to get connected and how to use the software . . .

SIGN ME UP!

If you actually want to get yourself on to the Internet, rather than using the school's or cybercafe's link, you will need to acquire the following hardware:

➡ Home computer, such as a PC, Mac, Amiga, or Atari
➡ A modem, the faster the better
➡ Standard home telephone line

You will also need:

➡ A service provider, a company that will sell you an Internet connection, just like the phone company rents you a regular phone line

And don't forget the software:

➡ Communications software to make your computer work with your modem; this is often built in to your system software already, or available from your service provider.

➡ Internet software that lets you e-mail, FTP and surf the Web; usually from the service provider, with much more available using FTP once you're online. There are plenty of programs that only do one thing, but the trend now is for Web

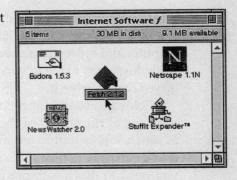

browsers like Netscape that do it all.

BASIC REQUIREMENTS

Just about any modern home computer will allow you to gain access to the Internet, though most surfers use an IBM-compatible PC or an Apple Macintosh. You

need a computer with a hard drive and plenty of RAM. Internet software can eat up memory, especially if graphics and video are involved. If you are downloading software via FTP, you're going to need a lot of hard drive space to store it.

Color and sound capability is ideal, but not essential. One of the virtues of the Web is that it gives you as much sophistication as your machine can manage; if you can only handle text and a little color, that's all you need to download; more powerful machines can take video clips and animated logos, too.

Online with a PC

There are no major problems using a PC to access the Internet. The only thing to remember when using a PC on the Net is that DOS-based programs aren't very good. You'll be better off with a Windows-based operating system if you have the option, especially Windows 95, which has Internet software already included.

Communications Software: TCP/IP software is what you need to connect your PC to the Net. A very good version comes standard with Windows 95 or OS/2 Warp, and there are equally good shareware programs, such as Trumpet Winsock, available from service providers and via FTP. NetDial will allow your modem to dial the number of your Point of Presence.

Internet Software: The two integrated Web browsers, Netscape and Mosaic, are standard; the first is by far the most popular. For FTP, use CuteFTP or WS_FTP. The best Telnet program is called CommNet. Try Eudora or Pegasus Mail for e-mail and the Free Agent newsreader for Usenet. IRC can be handled by WS_IRC. There are plenty of other programs available via FTP if you don't like these.

Online with a Mac

There is lots of Apple Macintosh Internet software available; because of the Mac's graphic-based approach, it has very few problems getting the best of the Net. Many programs now come in two versions, for regular Macs and for PowerMacs.

Communications Software: You need two programs to connect to your modem. MacTCP comes with all new Macs as part of System 7.5; it's also available from service providers. MacPPP or FreePPP dial your Point of Presence for you, and are available from shareware libraries and service providers. When the one you choose is installed, just open it up and click on "Open" to get connected right away.

Internet Software: Again, Netscape is everyone's favorite Web browser. For FTP use Fetch; for Usenet, try Newswatcher; for Telnet, try the Mac version of NCSA Telnet. Eudora is great for e-mail. Check out Homer for IRC. That's all there is to it!

Online with an Amiga

The Amiga is a pretty good Internet surfer—if you have enough memory. Workbench 2 and a hard drive are essential for anything more than e-mailing. The graphical browser AMosaic is fairly simple to use, but needs lots of RAM and the Magic User Interface in order to work.

The main problem is that some service providers do not support it. Shop around for one who does; once you've got AmiTCP you can FTP the other software you need and sign up with whoever you want.

Communications Software: AmiTCP is what you need, and it comes with some basic FTP and Telnet functions too.

Internet Software: AMosaic is the best Web browser; it's not as good as the PC or Mac versions yet (though there's an upgrade due) but can handle graphics and color. Alternatively there's ALynx. For simple e-mail use Elm; for Usenet try GRn; for IRC there's Grapevine. Others are available via FTP.

Online with an Atari

The Atari ST isn't well supported. Various Internet programs all seem to require different communications software, and even then they are clunky and text-only. You will need a hard disk, and probably a RAM upgrade too. Even more of a problem is that few service providers support the Atari ST.

Communications Software: This depends upon which Internet software you want to run. To use Lynx, you need the MiNT operating system and MiNTnet TCP/IP socket overlays. Alternatively, you should use the TCP/IP handler with the peculiar name KA9Q.

Internet Software: Oasis is a combined newsreader and e-mailer which is okay. Lynx is a text-only Web browser and e-mailer, and it's very clumsy to set up. Once it's up and running it's fine and logical, but doesn't support graphics, colors, and sounds. This is because, like most Atari software, it's been converted from an old PC DOS program. There have been rumors about more advanced Web browsers being developed, but nothing has appeared as yet.

Other computers

If you have an unusual or old computer, don't worry.
The chances are that, even if there isn't any software
around yet, there will be sooner or later. Keep watching the magazines devoted to your trusty old machine
for details. People have gotten online using the
strangest computers!

Some of the video game console manufacturers are
talking about releasing cartridges that will slot in like a
game to allow users to access the Internet. It's likely
that they will include communications and Internet
navigation software, which will be way cool. Video
game conversions will need their own keyboard
attachment to get the best from the Net; trying to key
in a URL or write e-mail by selecting every letter in
turn from an on-screen high-score chart is torture!
Keep your eyes peeled for developments as every man-
ufacturer tries to cash in on the Internet!

ALL ABOUT MODEMS

Modem: you've heard the word, but what does it mean? It stands for *mod*ulator/*dem*odulator. The smart little box of tricks that is a modem takes the signal sent out by your computer and modulates it, changing the message into a form that can be sent through a telephone

line. Then, when a message comes back, it demodu-
lates it back into computer-speak.

FIRST, CHOOSE YOUR MODEM

Here's a good rule for choosing any item of computer
equipment: buy the best thing you can afford. In the
case of a modem, you need the fastest unit possible.

Modem speeds are measured by the number of
computer bits per second (or *bps*) a unit can send and
receive. (Each character you type needs ten bits.) This
is known as the modem's *baud rate*.

The two recommended types of modem are known
as the V.32, which can send up to 14,400 bps, and the
V.34, which is twice as fast at 28,800 bps. It isn't worth
buying anything slower than a V.32 modem unless you
only want to use e-mail.

A typical V.32 modem costs about the same as a
basic video game console; a V.34 costs twice as much.
The faster your modem, the less time you need to
spend online, so in the long run the more expensive
modem can work out to be the better buy.

You'll need to decide what features you want on
your modem, too. There are two types: internal and
external. An internal modem has to be fitted inside
your computer, but that means it's out of the way and
it works off your computer's power supply. An external
modem sits nearby, so you get another box and a few
more cables cluttering up your desk. It also needs to be
plugged in, although some use batteries. However, you
do get to see the various flashing status lights on the
front, and you can move the modem from computer to
computer. Many modems also come with software that
will allow your computer to work as a fax machine.

CARELESS SURFING COSTS CASH

Once you've bought your modem, the only other expenses are paying the small monthly usage fee to your local Internet company—and the telephone bills. If your phone company provides free local calls, or does so at certain times, you won't have to worry about this. Also, if your connection is provided by your school or college, it won't be a problem.

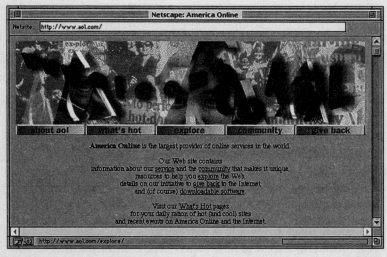

For the rest of us, it is important to remember those telephone bills. A few hints on keeping them to a minimum: first, the faster your modem, the less time you will waste waiting for a connection to come through or a long file to download. Second, sign up with a service provider that allows you to make local calls. In off-peak hours these should be free or only a few cents a minute—so only go surfing evenings and weekends, when phone rates are at their cheapest.

Some service providers supply customers with free or nearly free phone numbers to connect—then charge for access by the hour. Again, the faster your modem, the less time you will need to spend connected. There are several shareware timer programs available through FTP that will tell you how long you've been online. Many can be set to alert you after a certain time—such as when your allowance has just run out!

SIGN UP TO A SERVICE PROVIDER

The final link in the chain is the *service provider*, or the company that handles your local connection to the Internet. It may be an international company with links all over the world, or a friendly local outfit based just across town. Whichever you decide to go with, don't be afraid to shop around, if you can, and choose the exact service you want.

Find your provider

You find a good service provider the way you find any other person or company to provide a service. In some areas, of course, there will be only one local service provider, so you'll have no choice unless you want to connect to another company farther away.

If you know people who already have Internet access, ask them about their service providers. See which one the local cybercafe uses, too; they'll want the best service, so whomever they use is worth a try.

There are also magazines on just about every computer and on the Internet in general. Many of them include comprehensive lists of service providers for the whole country.

What to look for

You need a service provider who will allow you to connect to the Net cheaply, using a local call. Charges can mount up, so get the best deal you can.

Some service providers only offer e-mail, or restrict access to certain, controlled parts of the Internet. There are even some that don't offer World Wide Web access. Ask if there are any further charges for "extra" services; some providers bump up your bill for Web access or IRC, for example.

Ensure that they are able to provide the software for your particular make of computer, and support your speed and type of modem. There's no use signing on only to find you can't do anything! Amiga and Atari users should be especially careful to make sure they can be connected.

Try to discover how busy the service is, especially at peak times. Some providers are too popular for the number of machines they have, so in the evenings they are clogged and many users can't get on. If you can get a free trial (many of the larger companies offer them to persuade users to join up), look around and see how busy they are and what they offer.

Look for other special offers. Some providers even supply a little free storage space on the Web, so you can put together your own home page!

ONLINE SERVICE PROVIDERS

The commercial Online Service Providers (*OSPs*) offer a more structured and regulated service than regular Internet Service Providers. They are small, self-contained clubs that join the Internet, and they provide many extra services and chat rooms solely for their paying users. They have their own forums, as well as online shopping malls, sports and news services, FTP archives, and kids' chat areas.

Their software is usually easy to install and use, but may not have all the features of regular Net software. Some OSPs don't allow access to some of the weirder parts of the Internet; parents may prefer this. A few OSPs think that Web access is actually an optional extra and charge you more to use it.

OSPs often offer free or nearly free phone connections. However, they make up for this by charging a basic monthly fee that pays for a few hours, then charging a lot more for every extra hour. That's fine if you only have a little e-mail and Web surf once in a while; use the Net more than that, and it may prove expensive. Most people start with an OSP; many stay with them because OSPs offer just what they need; others, once bitten by the Internet bug, move on to a regular ISP.

The OSPs

Companies and the services they offer are improving and getting cheaper all the time. For up-to-date details on these companies, call them up and ask for a brochure. They often have special offers, so compare a few and choose the right one for you. There are many OSPs, but here are the most popular.

America Online: The world's largest service provider. AOL doesn't charge for most e-mail and provides full Net access. However, you cannot use IRC or Telnet. It also offers a bewildering amount of extra services, from the shopping areas and many exclusive home sites to extra message boards and chat rooms.

CompuServe: A truly worldwide service, Compu-Serve is available in 150 countries and is currently the biggest service provider in the U.S. Its habit of using numbers instead of names for one's address annoys people. It has in the past been expensive, although charges have dropped considerably. Web access feels like it's been tacked on, and it restricts access to certain areas of the Net. Its forums, newslines, and shopping mall are excellent. There is even an *offline* CompuServe magazine for subscribers!

Delphi: When its new graphic interface arrives Delphi may be more popular, but it's currently some-what old-fashioned and slow. Its databases and financial newslines are well liked, though, as well as its online multiplayer games, and Internet access is cheaper than most.

GEnie: Another old-fashioned network, GEnie doesn't have as many extras as other networks, though it does now have a graphical interface. It also doesn't currently support FTP except via e-mail.

IBM Global Network: Connected directly via IBM's

OS/2, this network is very easy to use. As its name implies, it is available in many countries. There are a full range of extra features, and it is cheaper and less likely to be busy than some other OSPs.

Microsoft Network: Possibly the simplest Net access there is, because it's all built into Windows 95. Since it's so new, some features are still being added and others aren't fully established. Every aspect is regulated and it is all a little expensive.

Netcom: An ISP that's grown into an OSP, Netcom is halfway between the two styles, and probably points the way to how future service providers may work. It allows full Internet access with its new NetCruiser interface, but also provides several newsfeeds and special forums, and charges by the hour.

Prodigy: Set up like a shopping mall, Prodigy is very popular across North America. It doesn't restrict Net access, though it can be an expensive extra. Its own

F
Y
I

America Online	1–800–827–6364
CompuServe	1–800–848–8199
Delphi	1–800–695–4005
GEnie	1–800–638–9636
IBM Global Network	1–800–775–5808
Microsoft Network	see the Windows 95 documentation
Netcom	1–800–501–8649
Prodigy	1–800–PRODIGY

forums and shopping services are great, and there are special areas for kids and even a Homework Helper service!

INTERNET SERVICE PROVIDERS

Full Internet Service Providers (*ISPs*) are generally newer than many OSPs, and better geared to modern Internet access. They do not usually have their own separate areas, and charge a flat monthly fee for access. (This is not true for a few, who charge like an OSP.) There aren't nearly as many special forums and shopping services, but you don't have to dig deep if you want to stay online. ISPs offer and can support the full range of sophisticated Net programs. They also allow access to every corner of the Internet at no extra charge. ISPs are recommended for users who want to get the most from the Net.

ISPs are not as structured or as regulated as OSPs. While there are national ISPs, many more tend to serve specific local areas. Your nearest city or town is likely to have one; just check in the phone book. Because they are nearby, they should offer local call access.

National ISPs either have local numbers across the country, or use SprintNet, which gives free calls in off-peak hours. These services are generally cheaper than those with a usage charge, provided you want to use the Net a lot. And you will!

F Y I • F Y I

Here are the largest national ISPs. There are also hundreds of local suppliers.

ANS	1–800–456–8267
BBN Planet Corporation	1–800–472–4565
Global Enterprise Services, Inc.	1–800–358–4437
Holonet	510–704–0160
Hypercon	1–800–652–2590
Imagine Communications Corporation	1–800–542–4499
Millenium	1–800–736–0122
Novalink	1–800–274–2814
The Portal	1–800–433–6444
PSI	1–800–827–7482
Questar Microsystems, Inc.	1–800–925–2140
SprintLink	1–800–817–7755
Traders' Connection	1–800–753–4223
YPN	1–800–NET–1133

HOW TO DO STUFF

So you've got your hardware and software. Now how do you use it?

TAKE IT EASY

You're probably pretty confused. There's the modem to plug in and figure out, communications software to install, and all of that Internet software, too. Take your time. Most of the best software these days is designed to be easy to use, but there are always exceptions.

Use the programs' Read Me files, and don't be afraid to call your service provider to ask for help if you get stuck on a technical point. If you mess up or your PC crashes, just restart the computer and try again.

HOW TO GET A FREE PROGRAM

The first thing you may want to do is use FTP to acquire some new programs. While most service providers supply something to help you navigate the Net, you're bound to need more. Don't be afraid to replace the programs you've been given with better ones, or newer versions. Some service providers are far from helpful, and only give you an FTP program and the address of where to go to get everything else. That's a pain, but it does get you using the Net right away! There are also lots of text files which contain manuals for newbies and instructions on every aspect of Net usage.

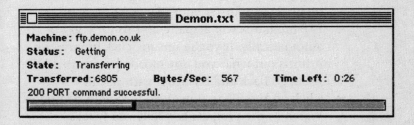

Using FTP
➡ Using your FTP program—they all work much the same—click on Open Location and type in the address of the FTP site. (Many are listed on pages 72–76; your service provider may also have its own.) Incidentally, web browsers like Netscape can also handle FTP, though they need

far more memory to run. On Netscape remember to include the ftp:// . . . prefix to the site's address.

➡ You'll need a password of some kind. Most use the Anonymous FTP system, so when they ask, your Username is "Anonymous," and your Password is your e-mail address. (This may have to be set up in the Open Location dialog.) Some sites are only available to authorized users; you'll only get in if you have the password.

➡ Once you are in, you'll be in an initial directory, often entitled "pub" (for public). Click on the sub-directory you need, such as "mac," for example. Keep clicking through the directories until you reach the program you want to download. (There may be a button to click on for Help, or a Read Me file, if you get stuck.)

➡ Decide whether to use ASCII (for downloading straight text) or binary (for programs, sound, pictures) to transfer your file; most modern FTP programs will actually do this for you automatically. If you're unsure, click binary; if it turns out what you downloaded is a garbled mess, go back and try again with ASCII!

➡ Click on the file to download it to your computer. Watch as the progress box tells you what's going on.

➡ Copy some more, or press Close Connection.

Back at your end

Many files are compressed so they can be stored in a small space; you might need to expand them once they've been downloaded. On a PC this will most likely mean using Winzip, on a Mac it'll be StuffIt, etc.

Such programs are available as shareware, and your service provider will be able to help if you don't have the right one.

HOW TO SEND E-MAIL

E-mail is very easy to figure out. After a few tries you, too, will be an e-mail expert, and will be firing off messages at the click of a mouse.

Before you log on

Launch your e-mail program and write your message first. If you connect to the Internet and *then* write your message, you're paying for your connection the whole time.

Create a signature. You can't sign e-mail with a pen, so your program lets you put a small note at the end of your e-mail. It's usually just a few lines: your name and e-mail address, plus a joke maybe. Some people take the trouble to create pictures using letters and punctuation. However, it's considered bad manners to have a signature longer than four lines.

Sending your message

Launch your Net connection. Make sure you have the correct address—most e-mail programs allow you to save

Address Books or Nickname files with all your regular contacts' addresses. When reading these instructions, remember that the exact terms your e-mail program uses may not be quite the same, but they will be similar.

➡ Choose "New Message." Type the destination under *To:* and your e-mail address under *From:*. Under *Subject:* write a short description of your message, e.g. Geeky Stuff or Hi Mom. If you want to send a copy to anyone, type their address under *Cc:* (or under *Bcc:* if you don't want them to know anyone else got a copy!).

➡ In the main area, type in your message. Use smileys and TLAs to keep it short.

➡ If you are sure everything is correct, press Send (or Send Later). When your modem comes online, press Connect.

➡ If you want to send a picture or another document with your e-mail, just select Attachments: and insert the names of the files (which you should have waiting on your hard drive).

➡ If you are writing several messages, you may want to send them all together, to save connection time. In such cases, Queue (or Send Later) the mail until you've written it all. Then go online and send it all at once.

Reading mail
Your e-mail program will tell you if you have new mail when you go online. Just call it up. It'll arrive in the In mailbox, where you'll be able to read all of the names of the senders and the subject headings. Click on one to open it. It'll come up in a window for you to read. Either reply, save, or delete it.

Writing e-mail

E-mails are a lot like postcards; they are generally short, chatty, and to the point. However, make sure you think about what you write and re-read it before you send it: it's very easy to say something you don't mean, and there's no way to change it afterwards.

If you're replying to a message, use the Reply feature instead. It'll open a new message window, usually with your pal's message highlighted as a quote (with a > at the start of each line). Snip out the sentences you don't

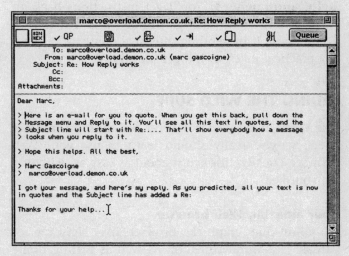

want to reply to, then add your responses. Note that the Subject: will now say "Re: [whatever it was originally]," but you can change it. Send it the usual way.

Mailing lists or Listservs

Mailing lists are like smaller versions of newsgroups, and are generally devoted to subjects that aren't quite popular enough to deserve a newsgroup. You "subscribe" to them by e-mailing their host computer and asking to join. Since some lists use slightly different ways of subscribing, it's best to ask for "info" or "help" in your first e-mail to the list. Once you're on, every message posted to the group will be sent to your e-mail address too. Most offer a digest version which will send all the postings in one file at the end of every day instead.

Anonymous messages

If you want to stay anonymous, send an e-mail to **help@anon.penet.fi** You'll get instructions back on how to route your message through this free service. Don't abuse it by sending offensive messages or playing practical jokes, or it'll get shut down.

RIDING THE WILD SURF

The World Wide Web is the real deal for most Internet users, so you really should learn to use your Web browser. Luckily, this is just about as easy as switching on your PC!

Your amazing Web browser

An all-in-one graphical browser like Netscape or Mosaic is a wonderful tool. As well as surfing home pages on the World Wide Web, you can often e-mail and collect news directly, and use it to launch your FTP or Telnet program automatically. A browser's also wonderfully easy to use, with point-and-click buttons and menus for everything.

What's an URL?

Every place on the Net can be reached via a *URL* or Uniform Resource Locator—its address. Web pages start **http://**, FTP sites start **ftp://**, a newsgroup will start **news:** (no slashes), and so on. The particular URL tells your browser the type of site, and where to go. For example, the World Wide Web address of Penguin Books is **http://www.penguin.com**

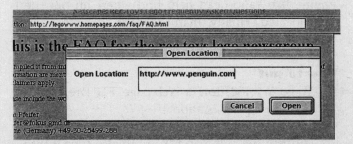

In a longer URL, each slash (/) denotes a new page into the site from the initial home page (like **http://www.penguin.com/usa/whatsnew.html**). This means that you can jump directly to specific pages within a site if you wish.

Finding an address

There are hundreds of Web addresses listed at the end of this book. You'll also see them on ads, at the bottom of magazine articles, on product packaging, all over the place. The many magazines devoted to the Internet are likely to be crammed with addresses of the hottest new sites. On the WWW you'll find plenty of sites that do nothing but provide links to addresses you want. If you can't track down a particular site, try the Yahoo directory or Lycos (see page 65). If they can't help, they'll know a place that can!

You must type the URL *exactly* as it is printed. Make sure capital letters are in the right format. If you can't get through, try again but only type the address as far as the previous /; keep retrying with a shorter and shorter address. It's also possible that you can't get through because a site has closed down. Many old addresses continue to provide direct links to their replacements for months after they've moved. A search engine like Yahoo can help find where an old site is now located. Finally, many student sites close down for vacations or because their owner has graduated.

How to surf

➡ To go to a location (a Web page, FTP site, etc.) click on Open Location.

➡ Type the full address into the box, then click to confirm the command. You can also type it into the empty Go to: box at the top of your browser. (Store your favorite sites in the Bookmarks or Hotlist file for easy recall.)

➡ Make sure it matches exactly the address you have. (If you're using Netscape, you can leave off the http:// part; that's the default setting.)

➡ That's all there is to it! Your browser will go to that location, if it is available and allowing access. You should be able to see it load in on the progress bar at the bottom of your browser.

➡ Once there, click on any of the highlighted words or the pictorial icons to surf to another page or site.

Troubleshooting

If you're not sure what to do on the Web, just click on a picture! Navigation buttons on your browser will also allow you to move back and forth between pages you've already visited.

Some sites are too busy at times to let everybody

in; you'll get a message telling you this. Go somewhere else, log off, and try again later.

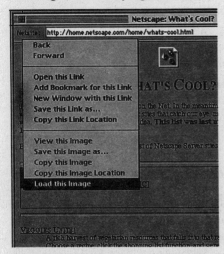

If you have a small computer or a slow connection, turn off the automatic picture loading, because huge images take a long time. You'll see the pictures come up as small generic icons instead. When you find something you do want to look at, you can click on the picture and load it. Particularly well-designed sites offer a text-only (or Low-Res) version.

To read USENET newsgroups, you'll need to enter the address of your news server in the browser's Preferences file (see page 60). Although you can Telnet with a browser, you'll need a proper Telnet program to do it.

TELNET

Some older sites don't yet support full Web access, so you have to Telnet to them. Use your Web browser, adding **telnet://** to the address, or a dedicated Telnet program. Note that most Telnet sites are extremely slow.

➡ Type in the address and press Enter. When prompted, type in the user name, then give your e-mail address as the password.

- If you are asked for a port number, type it into the Port: box in the Connect window of your software; the default is 23, but most sites will tell you what to use.
- Once you are in, type help or ? to get full instructions. Unfortunately, old-fashioned Telnet uses Unix instruction codes to move around, so get a list first. You should then be able to look at the files you want.

HOW TO JOIN A NEWSGROUP

Once you've e-mailed everyone you know, surfed through twenty-one thousand Web sites and gasped in awe at their amazing interactive contents, it's time to start contributing to Net culture. The best way to do this is by joining a newsgroup.

There are newsgroups devoted to thousands of different topics. Some are serious and scholarly, but the silly ones are more fun. (A list starts on page 78.)

News, please!

Don't forget the Netiquette relating to newsgroups (see page 67). On your first few visits just read the FAQ file, if there is one, and lurk in the background reading what's going on. Once you've gotten the idea, you can contribute.

Before you start using your newsreader, you'll need to enter the address of your service provider's news server (their own file full of newsgroup addresses, usually in the form **news.**[service provider's address]) in your newsreader's Preferences.

When you first launch your newsreader, it will

download a Full Group List of all of the newsgroups
available to you. It'll take a few minutes but you only
need to do it once. Then it's time to subscribe.

➡ Open up a New Group
Window. On your Full
Group List, click to
highlight a group you
want to join. From the
menus, select Subscribe.
Do this for each group
you want, then save
the window; call it
something like "My
Newsgroups." Next
time you launch your
newsreader, do so by
clicking on your group
list instead.

➡ Double click on the
group you want to read;
the number of unread
messages it holds should be alongside it. It'll
open up to reveal a list of the *threads* (the specific
discussions going on).

➡ Click on a message that looks interesting in order
to read it.

➡ Close the message, or use the up and down
arrows in the box's header to move to the next
message or thread.

➡ If you want to reply or start a new thread, use
Reply or New Message. Do it like e-mail, using
quoting, smileys, etc. Don't forget the Subject:
line; if you are replying to what someone has

already said, it'll be the same as the thread. Click Send. You can also send a private reply via e-mail to the person who posted; this guarantees they'll get to read it.

➥ *Cross-posting* (or *spamming*) means sending the same message to several newsgroups. It's frowned upon.

➥ Note that your own posting may not come up with all the others until the next time you launch your newsreader.

IT'S THE TLAS

In addition to smileys, there are also *TLAs*—Three Letter Acronyms. These stand for frequently used terms that are a pain to keep retyping; they keep messages shorter and faster to send. Some have been used for years; many more are new to the Internet. They might take a little getting used to, but soon you'll find yourself reading and writing them without thinking about it. They're only used in fun—and *never* in your homework!

FYI

Some of these have more or less than three letters, and some aren't even acronyms at all!

AFAICT	As far as I can tell
AFK	Away from my keyboard
B4	Before
BAK	Back at my keyboard
BCNU	Be seeing you
BFN	Bye for now
BRB	Be right back
BSF	But seriously, folks . . .

BTDT	Been there done that
BTW	By the way
CUL8R	See you later
DYJHIW	Don't you just hate it when . . .
EOF	End of file
FAQ	Frequently asked questions
FOAF	Friend of a friend
FOC	Free of charge
FWIW	For what it's worth
FYI	For your information
<G>	Grin!
GAL	Get a life
GIGO	Garbage in, garbage out
HHOJ	Ha ha, only joking
HHOS	Ha ha, only being serious
IAE	In any event
IMHO	In my humble opinion
IMNSHO	In my not so humble opinion
IMO	In my opinion
IOW	In other words
IRL	In real life
ISTM	It seems to me
ISTR	I seem to remember . . .
ITRW	In the real world
IYSWIM	If you see what I mean
JAM	Just a minute
L8R	Later
LMHO	Laughed my head off
LOL	Laughs out loud
MUG	Multi-user game
NALOPKT	Not a lot of people know that

NBD	No big deal
NRN	No reply necessary
OIC	Oh, I see
OMG	Oh my god!
OTOH	On the other hand
OTL	Out to lunch
OTT	Over the top
RFC	Request for comments
ROFL	Rolls on the floor laughing
RSN	Real soon now
RTFAQ	Read the FAQ file
RTFM	Read the manual
SITD	Still in the dark
SYL	See you later
TCB	The trouble came back!
TDM	Too darn many
TIA	Thanks in advance
TTFN	Ta-ta for now
TTYL	Talk to you later
TVM	Thank you very much
VR	Virtual reality
WRT	With regard to
WYSIWYG	What you see is what you get
YCT	Your comment to
YHM	You have mail
YMBJ	You must be joking
YMMV	Your mileage may vary

WHERE IS IT?

The Internet is now so huge it's possible to not know where to find FTP files or someone's home page. Luckily, there are a number of Web directories and automated search engines that are easy to use. The latest version of Netscape even has a built in search engine!

I said Yahoo!

The Yahoo system is a site designed to help lost Web users, where thousands of Web links join together. If you can't find a home page, ask Yahoo. (Or, for kid-related sites, Yahooligans.)

➡ Using your Web browser, go to **http://www. yahoo.com/** (or **http://www.yahooligans.com/**)

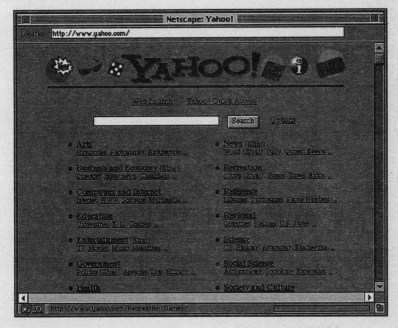

➡ On the main page, click on the topic you'd like. There are general ones (What's New, What's Cool, etc) and more specific (Entertainment, News, etc). The latest news headlines are also available.

➡ If you don't really know what you're looking for, type a word into the empty box and press Search. Note that the search is restricted to the Yahoo database.

➡ To customize your search, click on Options. Once at the Search page, type your topic into the main box, and click on all three of the boxes marked Find matches in . . . Press the Search button and cross your fingers!

➡ If you don't have any luck, Yahoo lets you jump to other Internet Directories, including . . .

Do you Lycos it?

Yahoo and similar sites are directories of links with some searching facilities. The Lycos search engine automatically crawls the Net adding new URLs. It also picks up excerpts from pages, headings, and other data to help in its searches. With more than ten million links, it covers close to 100 percent of the WWW. No wonder it calls itself "The Catalog of the Internet"! It can be very busy at times, because it's so good.

➡ Go to **http://www.lycos.com/**

➡ First, look in the general index. This is a list of the hottest sites, broken down by category just like a directory.

➡ If you don't find what you want, run a search. Type a relevant word or two into the box and click on Search. You'll get a list of every reference it found.

➡ Note that it isn't an intelligent creature. If you just type in "rock" you will get a list of both musical and geological home pages. Also, the more common a word, the slower the search will be.

Other search sites

These all work in much the same way. There are others, like Infoseek, which you have to pay to use.

Alta Vista: **http://www.altavista.digital.com/**
Excite: **http://www.excite.com/**
Global Network Navigator: **http://www.gnn.com/ gnn/gnn.html**
Harvest: **http://harvest.cs.colorado.edu/**
Webcrawler: **http://webcrawler.com/**
World Wide Yellow Pages: **http://www.yellow.com/**

NETIQUETTE

There are manners for the Internet, just like in real life. If you want people online to like and respect you, you have to follow Net etiquette—because if you don't, everyone will definitely let you know about it!

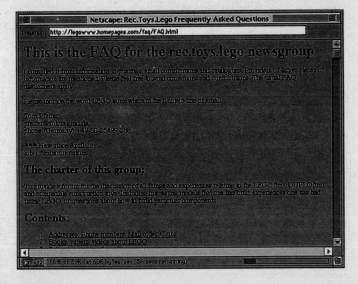

Online manners

If you ignore the following, you may get flamed!

Read the FAQ: There's nothing worse when you're having a chat than to have someone barge in and ask a dumb question. If you're joining a newsgroup or mailing list for the first time, read the Frequently Asked Questions file first, if there is one. If that doesn't answer your question, then you can feel free to ask the group.

The right place: Don't go to alt.basketweaving and start talking about Pearl Jam. In other words, make sure you're in the right place for the right topic.

Shhhhh!: If you type EVERYTHING IN CAPITALS LIKE THIS, that means you are shouting.

Repetition: If you're replying to someone, don't quote an enormous chunk of their message before your own comment. Snip it down to the pertinent points. Some people have to pay to download their e-mail messages—they don't want to spend money to read the same thing twice!

(Joke!): If you write something that is meant to be funny or sarcastic, use a smiley so your meaning is clear and can't be taken the wrong way. There are a lot of strangers with no sense of humor out there; make sure they know when you're kidding. And remember, not everything you read on a computer screen is true.

Other rules

If you are lucky enough to have Internet access at home, you probably won't need to be told about the following rules, but they're worth repeating. After all, it would be a shame if your mom and dad locked away your modem, wouldn't it?

Cost: Make sure the person who actually pays the telephone and Internet company bills knows when you are online. No matter how cheap your access, it still costs money.

Time: The Internet is a really neat place to hang out, but do your homework before you go surfing. The Net will still be there tomorrow or on the weekend.

Access: Don't forget that your Net link will tie up the phone while you're online. Any callers will get a busy signal. If you share the phone, it's best to work out a regular and specific time when you're online, so everyone knows not to call then.

Stay Streetwise: As in real life, when someone is rude or abusive, simply ignore them. If you think it's really serious or you are worried by anything, then you should *always tell an adult what's happened.*

EXPLORING THE NET

Here's where you'll learn what the Internet is all about, from the commercial corporate pages to the twisted underground inhabitants!

If you are online, especially if you've only got fifty-five minutes left on your cybercafe connection, you'll want to know how to access all the sites we've mentioned so far. Here they are, from free FTP files to bizarro Web sites. Each has its own address; dial in using the appropriate software and take your pick of the very best the Internet has to offer.

If you aren't online yet, it doesn't matter. Read and dream. Just sit back and take a trip around cyberspace.

Look, things change, okay?

When you get online, you might find you cannot access a few of these sites for yourself. They may have shut down or moved; it happens sometimes, but far less often than it used to. Or it may be because you have mistyped the address (or been given the wrong one in the first place). If retyping doesn't work and the old address doesn't link to the new site, try consulting an Internet directory.

Follow the links

In the directories which follow, you'll see this symbol ✛. It means that the address has links to many more sites. If you don't know where you want to go, head here first.

I WANT MY FTP

Whatever computer you use, there are FTP sites full of files for it. They include computer programs, text files with instructions on Net access, reference books, sounds, pictures, video clips, and so on. A few of these are Web sites (you'll spot them by their http:// addresses); start here using your browser, then switch to FTP when they tell you, or download direct if the site allows it.

Because some sites are universities or colleges that actually need to get some work done now and then, their public FTP areas are limited to a certain number of users a day. If you fail to get on to a site, look for a notice saying how many people have visited the site that day. Then, try again earlier the next day.

Software Collections
The Cross Platform Page: Shareware programs for PCs and Macs at **http://www.mcad.edu/guests/ ericb/xplat.html**

◈ FTP Interface: Links to hundreds of FTP sites start at **http://hoohoo.ncsa.uiuc.edu/ftp-interface.html**

The Great Freeware Page: Everything you download from here is free! **http://www.cris.com/~designty/**

Jumbo!: Massive selection of cool shareware, run by teenager Jon Conlon in New York. **http://www.jumbo.com/**

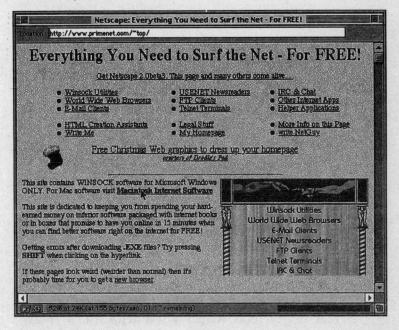

◈ The Shareware Resource Page: A database for searching the Net for the program you need. **http://execpc.com/~wmhogg/share.html**

SunSite: London Imperial College's immense shareware archives. **ftp://src.doc.ic.ac.uk/packages/**

PC Internet Software

Microsoft Windows 95: **http://www.windows. microsoft.com/**

✛ PC Software Links: A good place to search for that special utility is **http://www.uib.no/zoo/ wolf/daniel/pc-eng.html**

Ultimate Collection of Winsock Software: **http:// web.idirect.com/~tucows/software.html**

E-mail: Acquire the latest Eudora from **ftp://ftp. qualcomm.com/quest/eudora/windows/** Alternatively, try the powerful Pegasus from **ftp://risc.ua.edu/pub/network/pegasus/**

FTP: Download the program that'll help you download other programs from **ftp://papa. indstate.edu/winsock-1/ftp/**

Newsreader: FreeAgent can be downloaded from **ftp://ftp.forteinc.com/pub/forte/ free_agent/**

Telnet: CommNet is at **ftp://ftp.radient.com/**

Web browser: Get the latest version of Netscape from **ftp://ftp2.netscape.com/pub**

Mosaic's latest incarnation is at **ftp://ftp.ncsa. uiuc.edu/Web/Mosaic/Windows**

Mac Internet Software

Essential Mac Software: **http://www2.ios.com/ ~abtm/essential_mac_software.html**

Mac WWW Tools: **http://www.arpp.sfu.ca/tools/**

Well-Connected Mac: **http://www.macfaq.com/**

E-mail: Eudora's what you need, and it's at **ftp://ftp. qualcomm.com/quest/mac/eudora/**

FTP: Fetch yourself a copy of Fetch from **ftp://ftp.dartmouth.edu/pub/mac/**

Newsreader: Get your mitts on Newswatcher at

    ftp://ftp.acns.nwu.edu/pub/newswatcher/
Telnet: **ftp://ftp.ncsa.uiuc.edu/Mac/Telnet/**
Web browser: The mighty Netscape is yours from
    ftp://ftp2.netscape.com/netscape/mac/
The latest Mosaic is available at **ftp://ftp.ncsa.**
   uiuc.edu/Mac/Mosaic/

Amiga Software

✧ Amiga Link: Just for you Amiga users, there are a
   selection of hot links at **http://www.innotts.**
   co.uk/~garryh/amigalink.html

✧ Amiga Web Directory: **http://www.prairienet.**
   org/community/clubs/cucug/amiga.html

Aminet: Wuarchive has loads of Amiga material, at
   ftp://ftp.wustl.edu/~aminet

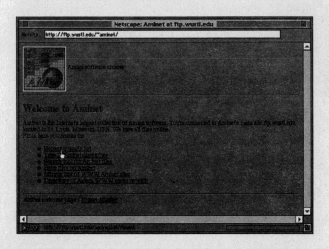

Newsreader: **ftp://src.doc.ic.ac.uk/aminet/**
   comm/uucp
Web browser: Grab your copy of AMosaic from
   ftp://ftp.demon.co.uk/pub/amiga/mosaic/

Atari Software

E-mail/newsreader: Oasis is available from **ftp://ftp. demon.co.uk/pub/atari/oasis**

Web browser: There are precious few FTP files available for the Atari. However, the Lynx web browser is; get it from **ftp://src.doc.ic.ac.uk/computing/ systems/atari/umich/Mint/Network/**

CAN WE TALK?

Do you want to get something off your chest? Here are political debates, philosophical mind-mangling, geeky chats about household appliances, and the Alicia Silverstone fan club. Before you post to any of

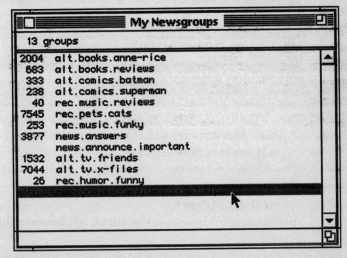

```
┌─────────────────────────────────────────────┐
│ □          ▓▓▓ My Newsgroups ▓▓▓          ▣ │
├─────────────────────────────────────────────┤
│   13 groups                                 │
│ ┌─────────────────────────────────────────┐ │
│ │ 2004   alt.books.anne-rice          ▲   │ │
│ │  683   alt.books.reviews                │ │
│ │  333   alt.comics.batman                │ │
│ │  238   alt.comics.superman              │ │
│ │   40   rec.music.reviews                │ │
│ │ 7545   rec.pets.cats                    │ │
│ │  253   rec.music.funky                  │ │
│ │ 3877   news.answers                     │ │
│ │        news.announce.important          │ │
│ │ 1532   alt.tv.friends                   │ │
│ │ 7044   alt.tv.x-files                   │ │
│ │   26   rec.humor.funny                  │ │
│ │ ▓▓▓▓▓▓▓▓▓▓▓▓▓▓▓▓▓▓▓▓▓▓▓▓▓▓▓▓▓           │ │
│ │                               ▶         │ │
│ │                                     ▼   │ │
│ └─────────────────────────────────────────┘ │
│ ┌─────────────────────────────────────┐  ▣ │
└─────────────────────────────────────────────┘
```

these groups *read the accompanying FAQ files*, if they are present. It'll save a lot of flaming later on.

(M) means that the group is "moderated."

Alternative
Aliens: They're here. **alt.alien.visitors**
Animaniacs: **alt.tv.animaniacs**
Arnie: He'll be back. **alt.fan.schwarzenegger**
Batman: **alt.comics.batman**

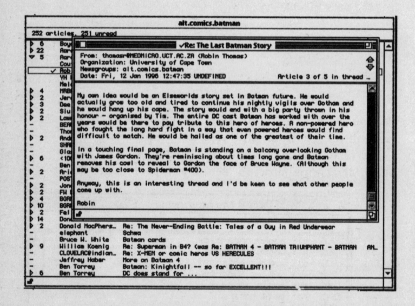

Batman Movies: And yuletide nightmares too.
alt.movies.tim-burton
The Bible: And on the seventh day . . . **alt.christnet.bible**
Bigfoot: **alt.bigfoot**
Boomerangs: Many happy returns. **alt.boomerang**

Breakfast Cereal: **alt.cereal**

British Comedy: Oh, I say, most amusing. **alt. comedy.british**

Burgers: **alt.food.mcdonalds**

Jim Carrey: Riddle me this. **alt.fan.jim-carrey**

Cats: **alt.animals.felines**

Christians: Praise be. **alt.christnet**

College Bowl Football: **alt.college.college-bowl**

Cows: Some people will talk about anything. **alt.cows.moo.moo.moo**

Dolphins: Good boy, Flipper. **alt.animals.dolphins**

Doom: **alt.games.doom**

Elvis: **alt.elvis.king**

Flaming: Stand back and watch the abuse fly. **alt.flame**

Freebies: Where to get 'em. **alt.consumers. free-stuff**

GI Joe: **alt.toys.gi-joe**

Hot Rod Racing: And they're off! **alt.hotrod**

Ice Cream: **alt.food.ice-cream**

IRC: **alt.irc.questions**

Jurassic Park: Run for your lives! **alt.books. crichton**

Kids: Friend central. **alt.kids-talk**

Stephen King: Leave the light on. **alt.books. stephen-king**

Looney Tunes: Duck season! Rabbit season! **alt. animation.warner-bros**

Math Homework: No cheating! **alt.algebrà.help**

Monster Movies: **alt.movies.monster**

Music: Hundreds of bands have their own newsgroups at **alt.music** . . . from Alice in Chains (**.aliceinchains**) and Beck (**.beck**) to TLC

(**.tlc**) and U2 (**.u2**). See if your idols are there too.

Newbies: The first place you should look. **alt.newbie**

Origami: **alt.arts.origami**

Peanuts: Curse you, Red Baron! **alt.comics.peanuts**

Pen Pals: What do you like to do? **alt.kids-talk. penpals**

Pet Fish: **alt.aquaria**

Brad Pitt: **alt.fan.brad-pitt**

Power Rangers: **alt.fan.power-rangers**

Rabbits: **alt.pets.rabbits**

Rap Music: **alt.rap**

Shareware: Specifically for young people. **alt.comp. shareware.for-kids**

The Simpsons: I'm all Itchy and Scratchy. **alt.tv. simpsons**

Skateboarding: Excellent! **alt.skate-board**

Sonic the Hedgehog: **alt.fan.sonic-hedgehog**

Sports: everything from **alt.sports.baseball** to **alt.sport.lasertag** is covered; just pick your favorite. There are also forums devoted to specific teams.

Stereograms: **alt.3d.sirds**

Superman: All the news from the Daily Planet. **alt.comics.superman**

Teddy Bears: **alt.collecting.teddy-bears**

Teenage Chat: **alt.teens**

Television: Everything from Barney (**alt.tv.barney**) to the X-Files (**alt.tv.x-files**) and a hundred other shows in between.

Three Stooges: **alt.comedy.slapstick.3-stooges**

Transformers: It's a can of asparagus. It's a robot! **alt.toys.transformers**

Video Games: **alt.video.games.reviews**

Computer

All sorts of computer topics are under the **comp.** heading. Here are some of the more introductory groups. Check your Full Group List for their expert level spinoffs.

Amiga: **comp.sys.amiga.introduction**
Amiga Games: **comp.sys.amiga.games**
Atari: **comp.sys.atari.st**
Mac: **comp.sys.mac.misc**
Mac Games: **comp.sys.mac.games.misc**
PC: **comp.sys.ibm.pc.misc**
PC Games: **comp.sys.ibm.pc.games.misc**

Miscellaneous

Kids' Groups: All of the serious newsgroups concerning children are in the **misc.kids.** area, though many are *about* young people, rather than *for* them.

Computers for Kids: **misc.kids.computer**
Home Schooling: **misc.education.home-school.misc**
Kids: **misc.kids**
Kids' Groups: **misc.kids.info** (M)
Kids on Vacation: **misc.kids.vacation**
Sick Kids: **misc.kids.health**
Stuff for Kids: **misc.kids.consumers**

Newsgroups on News

The **news.** group is for those who organize the USENET, and for interested observers. Most of the newsgroup titles make their subjects obvious. Newbies should check these out:

news.announce.important (M)
news.announce.newgroups (M)
news.announce.newusers (M)
news.answers
news.groups
news.misc (M)
news.newusers.questions

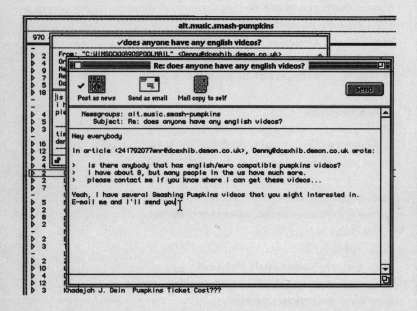

Recreation
Animation: **rec.arts.animation**
Bicycles: **rec.bicycles.misc**
Board Games: **rec.games.board**
Book Reviews: **rec.arts.books.reviews** (M)
Books for Kids: **rec.arts.books.childrens**

Boy Scouts: **rec.scouting**
Chess: Make your move to **rec.games.chess**
Chocolate: **rec.food.chocolate**
Cinema: **rec.arts.movies**
Comic Books: **rec.arts.comics.info** (M)
Disney Cartoons: **rec.arts.disney.animation**
Juggling: **rec.juggling**
Lord of the Rings: **rec.arts.books.tolkien**
Magic Cards: **rec.games.trading-cards.magic.misc**
Movie Reviews: **rec.arts.movies.reviews** (M)
Music: Just like **alt.music** . . . only with more
    established bands and genres, from the Grateful
    Dead to REM, and rock 'n' roll to industrial.
    rec.music
Pets: Don't forget to clean that litter box. **rec.pets**
Record Reviews: **rec.music.reviews** (M)
Role-playing Games: **rec.games.frp.misc**
Scouting: **rec.scouting**
SF Reviews: **rec.arts.sf.reviews** (M)
Sports: More sports newsgroups, from **rec.sport.**
    archery to **rec.sport.volleyball**, with football,
    hockey, tennis, and many more.
Star Trek: **rec.arts.startrek.info** (M)
Star Wars: **rec.arts.sf.starwars.info** (M)
Toys: Something to play with. **rec.toys.misc**
TV Soaps: **rec.arts.tv.soaps.misc**
Wild Animals: Grrrrrr. **rec.animals.wildlife**

MAIL ME!

There are many more mailing lists than we can detail
here, with new ones starting every day. To see if your
hobby has its own list, check Stephanie da Silva's

comprehensive catalog at **http://www.NeoSoft.com/internet/paml/** and on **news.lists** or e-mail **mail-server@nisc.sri.com** with the message "send netinfo/interest-groups" (be warned: the file you get back will be enormous!).

A.Word.A.Day: Every morning you'll receive a new word and its definition, after e-mailing **wsmith @wordsmith.org**

Arachnid: Owners of tarantulas or scorpions chat on **majordomo@bga.com**

Balloon Sculpting: **balloon-request@cvs. rochester.edu**

Baseball Chat: To join this forum for baseball fans, send a blank e-mail message to **info @plaidworks.com**

Bedrock Online: The Flintstones list keeps on rocking from **listserv@netcom.com**

Bible: The busy Bible Study mailing list is available from **majordomo@virginia.edu**

Bicycle: **listproc@yukon.cren.org**

Children's Writing: The list for writers and illustrators of children's books is at **majordomo@lists.mindspring.com**

Chocolate: Share your favorites with **listserv@idma.com**

Clarissa: Fans of the TV show *Clarissa Explains It All* gather at **clarissa-request@tcp.com**

Classical Music: **classical-request@webcom.com**

Dallas Cowboys: **cowboys-request@emmitt.dseg.ti.com**

Dinosaur: **listproc@lepomis.psych.upenn.edu**; in the body of the message put "Subscribe Dinosaur [yourname]"

Fruit of the Day: Every night a new message will inform what the official fruit of the day will be. E-mail **fotd-request@cs.umd.edu** with the message "info"

Ghost Stories: This list sends out one new ghost story each day from **ghost-stories-request@netcom.com**

Hockey Chat: **info@plaidworks.com**

Kids' Books: Reviews of children's books are sent out regularly from **kidsbooks-request@armory.com**

Kites: **kites-request@harvard.edu**

Magic: **magic-request@maillist.crd.ge.com**

Metallica: **metallica-request@thinkage.com**

Pen Pals: Smart, moderated list of pen pals for children, from **pen-pals-request@mainstream.com**

The Recipe Page: Every Sunday you'll get a newsletter full of food stuff, from **CAPCO@magnum.wpe.com**

Rocks and Fossils: **majordomo@world.std.com**
SF-Lovers: Science fiction fans gather at **sf-lovers-request@rutgers.edu**
Sonic: **majordomo@lists.mv.net**
Spider-Man: **majordomo@listserv.intellinet.com**
X-Files: **listproc@chaos.taylored.com**

Starting Your Own List

For instructions on how to set up your own mailing list on a subject that isn't yet covered, contact **listserv @bitnic.educom.edu**

E-MAIL CONNECTIONS

Although most e-mail addresses follow a similar format, some of the older services have their own way of doing things. This can make communicating troublesome unless you are aware of the differences.

In all of these, [name] is the other person's user name and [address] is your full e-mail address.

	Send to	Received as
America Online:	[name]@aol.com	[address]
CompuServe:	[00000.0000]@ compuserve.com*	INTERNET: [address]
Delphi:	[name]@delphi.com	IN%"[address]
GEnie:	[name]@genie.geis.com	[address]@inet#
Prodigy:	[name]@prodigy.com	your provider: [your name]

Note: Although a CompuServe internal address is a number divided by a comma (e.g., 12345,6789), replace the comma with a period when you send mail there.

WHAT'S ON TELNET?

Not as much as there used to be. Many locations are turning their resources into fully graphical World Wide Web sites instead. On the other hand, there are still some computers which are only accessible via Telnet, so it's worth it to look around.

In all of the following addresses, the word following the colon (:) is the password or user name you need to use to access the site. If you're using a dedicated Telnet program, ignore the **telnet://** part; that's only used by an integrated Web browser like Netscape.

Archie: Operate the Archie search engine to find some choice FTP files via **telnet://archie.ans.net: archie**

Cookie Servier: That's a "fortune cookie," a random piece of homespun wisdom every time you telnet into **telnet://argo.temple. edu: 12345**

Electronic News Stand: **telnet://enews.com: news**

E-Mail Addresses: A very comprehensive database, and one that is updated very regularly to boot. **telnet://nri.reston.va.us** and set the port to= 20185 to use the Knowbot that will guide you through the directory.

Friends and Partners: This was set up so that Russians and Americans could talk to each other, but other people sometimes join in; **telnet://solar.rtd. utk.edu: friends**

HENSA: That's the well-stocked Higher Education National Software Archive, and it's at **telnet:// micros.hensa.ac.uk: hensa**

InterNIC: A host of services designed to help you get started as an Internet newbie. Call up the information you need through **telnet://ds. internic.net: guest**

Liberty: The Liberty server at Washington & Lee University in Virginia: **telnet://liberty.uc. wlu.edu**

NASA Extragalactic Database: Quite simply the best thing on Telnet, and it's at **telnet://denver. ipac.caltech.edu: ned**

National Archaeological Database: If you like digging for old bones: **telnet://cast.uark.edu: nadb**

Online Games Server: Even in these Doom-dominated days, there are people out there pretending to be wizards and warriors using only a series of typed-in commands. Join them at **telnet://castor.tat. physic.uni-tuebingen.de: games**

Princeton University Library: Especially good for material on ancient history, check **telnet:// pucable.princeton.edu: call 500**

SunSite: London Imperial College's immense FTP archives, with programs for most machines. **telnet://src.doc.ic.ac.uk: sources**

World Wide Web: See where it all started, CERN headquarters in Switzerland, at **telnet://info. cern.ch**

WORLD WIDE WEB SITES

You want to know what the Internet is really like? Just look at these sites. Some are academic, many more are full of fun things to read and do. And then there

are the stupid ones—which are often the most fun!

A few sites may be gone, though most of the good ones only go off-line for a short time while they are updated and improved. If there's nothing there, check again in a week.

One last word: If you don't like where you are, just click again and continue surfing.

NEWBIES START HERE

Everything You Need: Free programs for every aspect of Net navigation can be found at **http://www. primenet.com/~tcp**

✧ Imajika's Guide to New Users: **http://www. sjr.com/sjr/www/bs**

Internet: That tedious history lesson about how the Net came to be can be revisited at **http://www.lysator.liu.se/etexts/ the_internet.html**

✧ Internet 101: **http://www.info.apple.com/ wwcc/internet-brochure.teaser.html**

✧ Nuggets for Newbies: **http://www.cccd.edu/ newbie.html**

Understanding the Internet: **http://www.screen. com/start**

INTERNET LATEST

Best of the Web Awards: From **http://wings. buffalo.edu/contest**

CERN: The home of the Web's creators. **http:// www.cern.ch**

Creating Net Sites: Sooner or later, everyone thinks

about putting up their own home page. Get
started at **http://home.netscape.com/assist/
net_sites**

Cybercafes: Find your nearest computers 'n' coffee
place at **http://www.easynet.co.uk/pages/
cafe/ccafe.htm**

Finding People on the Internet: **http://www.nova.
edu/Inter-Links/**

HTML Learners: Create your own home pages!
**http://www.ncsa.uiuc.edu/demoweb/
html-primer.html**

✦ Internet Search Tools: Can't find that real cool site?
Forgotten Yahoo's URL? Try the essential
**http://www.earthlink.net/free/bigbee/
webdocs/links/html**

Today's Cool Site: **http://cool.infi.net/**

The World Wide Web Initiative: The home of the
WWW, full of technical information for
inquisitive Netheads. **http://www.w3.org/**

✦ World Wide Web Wanderer: **http://www.
netgen.com/info/growth.html**

YOUNG NET

The following are specifically for children and cool
young Netheads.

Children's Internet

Buckman School, Room 100: The first online net-cam
based in a schoolroom: **http://buckman.pps.
k12.or.us/picturecam.html**

✦ Cyberhaunts for Kids: **http://www.woodwind.
com:80/cyberkids/**

Hillside Elementary School: Say hi! to the coolest kids online, at **http://hillside.coled.umn.edu/**

✧ Interesting Places for Kids: **http://www. crc.ricoh.com/people/steve/kids.html**

Kiddin' Around: A great gateway for all ages at **http://alexia.lis.uiuc.edu/~watts/kiddin. html**

KIDOPEDIA: An encyclopedia for children, written by children. Contribute at **http://rdz.stjohns. edu/kidopedia/**

KidPub: Write and post your own stories, or read everybody else's, at **http://escrime.en-garde. com:80/kidpub/**

✧ Kids' Corner: Activities for younger children, with puzzles, pictures, and surfing links, at **http:// www.ot.com:80/kids/**

✧ Kids' Web: All kinds of interesting topics here,

and some educational stuff too. **http://www.
npac.syr.edu:80/textbook/kidsweb/**

Spoot's Page: A home page designed by twelve-year-
old Nicky Moser! **http://daugherty.rice.edu/
Nicky/nicky.html**

◈ Uncle Bob's Kids' Page: The Net's own lovable
old grandpa, with links to fun places for young
Netheads; say hi at **http://gagme.wwa.com/
~boba/kids.html**

Virtual Exhibits on the WWW: Find the interactive
museum on the subject you want, starting
at **http://library.wustl.edu/~prietto/
exhibits/**

Youth, Education & Schools: The online magazine
that makes learning fun (ahem) is at **http://
www.oneworld.org/yes.html**

Fun Stuff

Animal Information Database: SeaWorld is a huge
theme park, and this is their fascinating
educational site. **http://www.bev.net/
education/SeaWorld/homepage.html**

◈ The Big Busy House: Find out how your favorite
books got published or ride the Taxi to follow
the cool kids' links from **http://www.
harpercollins.com/kids/**

Build-a-Monster: **http://www.rahul.net/cgi-bin/
renoir-cgi-bin/monster.pl**

Crayola: **http://www.crayola.com/crayola/**

Electric Postcard: Send an individual e-mail postcard
from **http://postcards.www.media.mit.edu/
Postcards/**

Exploratorium Museum: San Francisco online

museum with loads of interactive exhibits:
http://www.exploratorium.edu/

Field Museum of Natural History, Chicago: Take a tour through the DNA to Dinosaurs exhibit in this top American museum: **http://www.bvis. uic.edu/museum/exhibits/EXHIBITS.html**

Games Kids Play: **http://www.corpcomm.net/ ~gnieboer/gamehome.htm**

Global Show & Tell: Show off what you got to young Net users all around the planet! **http://emma. manymedia.com:80/show-n-tell/**

The Happiest Home Page on Earth: Everything you ever wanted to know about Disneyland is right here at **http://thoth.stetson.edu/users/ Bill_Sawyer/Disney.html**

HypArt: Contribute to the biggest painting in the world; start scribbling at **http://rzsun01. rrz.uni-hamburg.de/cgi-bin/HypArt.sh**

Kids on Site: Take a trip around an interactive

building site; hard hats are optional at **http://
www.digikids.com/KOS/KOSKIDS.HTML**

Kinetic City Super Crew: Online science games with
ALEC the smart computer. **http://www.aaas.
org/EHR/kcsuper.html**

My Page for Sam: Sam Shemitz's dad stuck up this
page for him. It's pretty cute; peek at **http://
deepthought.armory.com/~tachyon/
page4sam.html**

The North Pole: **http://north.pole.org/santa**

The Refrigerator: Stick your own pictures up for all to
see at **http://web.aimnet.com/~jennings/
refrigerator/index.html**

Theodore Tugboat: Charming interactive storybook;
chug along to **http://www.cochran.com/
tt.html**

Tigger's Children's Shareware Page: The hottest
programs for the coolest kids start at **http://
remarque.berkeley.edu/~tigger/sw-kids.html**

Time for Kids: The young version of Time magazine is
now online at (careful with this!) **http://www.
pathfinder.com/@@MdNE2BC9swMAQLgd/
TFK/index.html**

AND HERE WE HAVE . . .
SCIENCE MUSEUMS

Online museums can be great places to explore, especially now that some have interactive exhibitions on
their Web pages. And, yes, they can help you with your
homework!

The Cowboy Hall of Fame: **http://www.
horseworld.com/nchf/chfhome.html**

Eureka Children's Museum: **http://www.demon. co.uk/eureka/**

EXPO Ticket Office: Astonishing interactive exhibitions on a thousand different subjects; take this cool tour from **http://sunsite.unc.edu/ expo/ticket_office.html**

Franklin Institute Science Museum: Another great point-and-click interactive tour, at **http://sln. fi.edu/**

✧ History of Science: Museums: Links to dozens of cool exhibits, starting at **http://aibn55.astro. uni-bonn.de:8000/~pbrosche/hist_sci/ hs_mus.html**

National Civil Rights Museum: **http://www. magibox.net/~ncrm/**

✧ Natural History Museum, London: One of the best British museums, with plenty of information and links to other sites; enter at **http://www.nhm. ac.uk/**

Royal Tyrrell Museum: More dinosaurs! **http:// www.cuug.ab.ca:8001/VT/Tyrrell/**

✧ The Smithsonian: **http://www.si.edu/**

UCMP Time Machine: An awesome interactive journey through the Earth's history, courtesy of the California Museum of Paleontology; climb aboard at **http://ucmpl.berkeley.edu/timeform.html**

United States Civil War Center: **http://www. cwc.lsu.edu**

READ ME
BOOKS AND COMICS

Here are some favorite sites devoted to books and authors.

Books

⟡ Author! Author!: Find your favorite scribbler through the literate links at **http://www. greyware.com/authors/**

⟡ Children's Literature Web Guide: The complete guide to kids' books on the Net; start at **http://www.ucalgary.ca/~dkbrown/ index.html**

⟡ Home Page of Children's Literature: Reviews of thousands of the best books, at **http://www. parentsplace.com/readroom/index.html**

Library of Congress: **http://lcweb.loc.gov/ homepage/lchp.html**

The Oz Page: **http://www.best.com/~tiktok/**

Penguin Books: Not that we're biased, but . . . **http://www.penguin.com**

Mark Twain Library: Sail down the Mississippi with Huck and friends at **http://hydor.colorado. edu/twain/**

Comics

Calvin & Hobbes Archive: **http://www.eng.
hawaii.edu/Contribs/justin/Archive/
Index.html**

✧ Comix 'n' Stuff: **http://www.phlab.missouri.
edu/HOMES/c617145_www/comix.html**

The Far Side Directory: Delve into the warped depths
of Gary Larson's brain at **http://www.acm.uiuc.
edu/rml/Gifs/Farside/**

Superman Home Page: **http://web.syr.edu/
~ajgould/superman.html**

United Media Comic Strip: All the daily favorites,
from Peanuts to Marmaduke, are at **http://www.
unitedmedia.com/comics/**

Wayne Manor: **http://www.books.com/batman/
batman1.htm**

IS IT THE RIGHT WAY UP?
ART MUSEUMS

Gasp at a Van Gogh, marvel at a Manet and ponder a
Picasso—or, for *real* works of art, jump straight to the
graffiti pages!

Galleries on the Net

✧ Art on the Net: **http://www.art.net/**

The Louvre: **http://www.paris.org:80/Musees/
Louvre/**

Native American Art Gallery: **http://www.infoI.
com/NAAG/**

✧ Voice of the Shuttle: The very first place to look for
all things arty on the Net; check **http://
humatias.ucsb.edu/shuttle/art.html**

The WebMuseum: The best gallery of the online world, full of art masterpieces; start at **http://www.emf.net/louvre/**

Popular Art

Computer Art Gallery: Some awesome new computer-generated pictures are at **http://www.ior.com/~elie/compart.htm**

The Graffiti Wall: **http://www.cnet.com/home/bowman/graffiti.html**

Grafix: **http://pncl.co.uk/subs/rsmith/rsmith.html**

Photo Net: All the info on cameras and photography, with a massive online gallery, at **http://www-swiss.al.mlt.edu/phllg/photo/**

Vern's SIRDS Gallery: More 3-D stereograms than your brain can contain, at **http://www.sirds.com/**

IT'S ONLY A MOVIE!

Film pages fall into two broad categories: official movie company pages, which offer glimpses of forthcoming movie blockbusters, sometimes with trailers as video clips; and fan-based pages of ravings on cult movies, reviews, or general film chat.

Reviews and Information

⟡ The Internet Movie Database: A massive mountain of movie information, from reader reviews to links to other sites, is at **http://www.cm.cf.ac.uk/Movies/welcome.html**

Mark's Godzilla Page: **http://www.ama.caltech.**

edu/users/mrm/godzilla.html

Martial Arts: Did you study at the school of Shao Lin? **http://www.primenet.com/~martial/**

Mr. Showbiz: For the latest in hot entertainment news and comment, check out **http://web3. starwave.com/showbiz**

Mondo Bondo: All things 007, shaken not stirred, are at **http://www.delphi.com/entment/ motnpict/view/mondo.htm**

Movie Clichés: Find out why spaceships make noises in the silent vacuum of space, and much more at the hilarious **http://www.well.com/user/ vertigo/cliches.html**

✧ MovieWeb: You watch movies? You need the essential reviews and features at **http:// movieweb.com/movie/movie.html**

Silver Screen Cowboys: **http://www.cowboypal. com/**

Teen Movie Critic: Young Roger Davidson gives his personal view on the new releases at **http:// www.dreamagic.com/roger/teencritic.html**

Movies and Movie Studios

Batman Forever: Access pictures, sounds, and film clips at **http://www.batmanforever.com/**

Disney/Buena Vista Movieplex: **http://www. disney.com/**

✧ The Disney Link: **http://falcon.jmu.edu/ ~pollarpe/other-disney.html**

Lucasfilm: The all-new Star Wars movie is coming at last; get the latest from **http://bantha.pc.cc. cmu.edu/LUCASFILM/**

MCA/Universal Cyberwalk: **http://www.mca.com/**

MGM/United Artists: Visit the Lion's Den, especially

the *Hackers* site (infamous for being modified by real hackers!), at **http://www.mgmua.com/ MGM/index.html**

Paramount Pictures: **http://www.paramount.com/**

Sony Corporation: **http://www.spe.sony.com/ Pictures/SonyMovies/index.html**

Star Trek Generations: For the most recent installment, beam down to **http://generations. viacom.com/**

Star Wars: More trivia than you could possibly imagine at a fan site far, far away, at **http:// www.pitt.edu/~mprst6/starwars.html**

Sundance Institute: Seek out the stars of tomorrow at **http://cybermart.com/sundance/institute/**

Twentieth Century Fox: You must check out the

awesome interactive Star Wars site with scripts, stills, clips, and more, at **http://www.tcfhe.com**

Stars' Home Pages

Sandra Bullock: **http://weber.u.washington.edu/ ~louie/sandra.html**

Jim Carrey: **http://www.halcyon.com/browner/**

Anna Chlumsky: Mac's little friend from *My Girl* gets her own page at **http://www.kuai.se/ ~knorman/mygirl/homepage.html**

Harrison Ford: **http://www.mit.edu:8001/ people/lpchao/harrison.ford.html**

KeanuNet: **http://www.users.interport.net/ ~eperkins/**

Val Kilmer: **http://www.tc.cornell.edu/~cat/ pages/**

Brad Pitt: **http://www.sils.umich.edu/~mortal/ bradpitt/bradpitt.html**

Alicia Silverstone: **http://www.vt.com/~mickey/
Alicia/alicia.html**

WATCH THE NET
TELEVISION

If your own favorite program isn't listed here, check
out the enormous TV Net Ultimate TV List at **http://
tvnet.com/UTVL/utvl.html** for data on every single
TV show ever shown in the entire world ever (almost).

Reviews and Information

Discovery Channel: A little graphics heavy, but an
excellent site that makes learning through
watching TV a fun thing to do. **http://www.
discovery.com/**

Dominion: The Science Fiction Channel's
alien-packed home pages, at **http://www.
scifi.com/**

✛ Nerd World TV Celebs: More than twenty
thousand links, so when we say "All your stars
are here . . ." we really mean it! **http://
challenge.tiac.net/users/dstein/nw1030.
html**

✧ Science Fiction TV: **http://www.nova.edu/ Inter-Links/scifi.html**

✧ Tardis TV: You want information on a TV show, any TV show? Tune in to **http://src.doc.ic.ac. uk/public/media/tv/collections/tardis/ index.html**

✧ TV Chat: Several arenas, split into soaps, sci-fi, drama, and more, where you can talk with like-minded tube-watchers, at **http://tvnet.com/ TVChat/chat.html**

TV Episode Guide: **http://www.tardis.ed.ac.uk/ ~dave/guides/index.html**

✧ Yahoo's Television Links: **http://www. yahoo.com/Entertainment/Television/ Shows/**

Funny Stuff

Cathouse British Comedy Pages: Huge site dedicated to some of the best comedy in the world. **http://cathouse.org:8000/BritishComedy/**

Comedy Shows: **http://www.tvtrecords.com/ tvbytes/comedy.html**

Friends: **http://www.uidaho.edu/~hodg8931/**

The Ren & Stimpy Page: **http://www.cris.com:80/ ~lkarper/rands.html**

Saturday Night Live: It's a floorwax. It's a dessert topping. It's an old SNL routine. **http://www. cis.ohiostate.edu/hypertext/faq/usenet/tv/ sat-night-live/top.html**

The Simpsons Archive: **http://www.digimark.net/ TheSimpsons/**

✧ The Sitcom Page: **http://pmwww.cs.vu.nl/ service/sitcoms/**

More TV

Baywatch: **http://baywatch.compuserve.com/**

Dr. Who: **http://www.users.interport.net/
~cybermen/home.html**

FBI X-Files Division: Inexplicable goings-on with
Mulder and Scully at **http://www.delphi.com/
XFiles/**

50 Best Commercials: **http://www.adage.com/
Features/Commercials/**

Gladiators: **http://www.cityscape.co.uk/users/
ak90/index.html**

Gumby: Even download the theme song, if you must,
from **http://www.xnet.com/~gumby/
gumby.html**

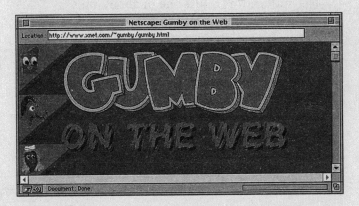

Jeopardy: **http://www.spe.sony.com/Pictures/
tv/jeopardy/jeopardy.html**

Lois & Clark: **http://www.creacon.com/LNC/**

The Ricki Lake Show: **http://www.spe.sony.com/
Pictures/tv/rickilake/ricki.html**

MTV: Newly revived home pages of the 24-hour

music channel; warning: huge graphics!
http://www.mtv.com/
The Muppets: Unofficial but packed with facts
on Kermit and the gang, at **http://www.
ncsa.uiuc.edu/VR/BS/Muppets/muppets.
html**
Power Rangers: **http://kilp.media.mit.edu:8001/
power/homepage.html**
Rugrats: **http://www.gfi.net/azog/rugrats/**
✛ Soap Links: **http://www.cts.com/~jeffmj/
soaps.html**
Star Trek: TNG: Make it so at **http://www.ugcs.
caltech.edu/~werdna/sttng/**
Star Trek Universe: The most popular show with
Net-surfers, this is just one of about, oh,
three million Trekker sites; boldly go to
**http://www.algonet.se/~quark/st.
html**

HERE WE ARE NOW, ENTERTAIN US ENTERTAINMENT

Not **alt.music.nirvana**, but a large selection of pages
concerned with entertainment, from stand-up comedi-
ans to more futuristic Web games.

Futuristic Fun
Conquest: An epic interactive medieval war game;
rule the world from **http://misha.net/
~conquest/conq.html**
Ferret Frenzy: Pick the weasel that will win the race
at **http://www.delphi.co.uk/delphi/
interactive/ferrets/intro.html**

Letter RIP: A grisly variation on Hangman with a zombie who loses a limb every time you make a mistake! **http://www.dtd.com/rip**

Murder on the Menu: An interactive murder mystery game; spot the killer at **http://www.best.com/ ~dglazer/murder/**

Puzzle Page: Interactive puzzles to make your brain ache; go figure at **http://www.tne.com/ ~janus/puzzle/ppage.htm**

The Riddler: Hunt the Net for hidden clues to the big prize; start at **http://www.riddler.com**

The Spot: A cool house with "real people" is the theme of the first Net soap opera; tune in at **http://www. thespot.com/**

The Tele-Garden: A remote-controlled gardening droid is under your control at **http://www.usc. edu/dept/grden/**

Virtual Town: A computerized community; explore at your leisure, but be warned: the graphics are huge! **http://wwwcsif.cs.ucdavis.edu/virt-town/town-graphic.html**

Lifestyle

Autographs: **http://www.sofcom.com.au/ Autographs/index.html**

Cereal Fashions: Yes, clothes made out of breakfast cereal! **http://198.3.117.222/fashion.html**

CNN Style News: What all the supermodels are wearing this season, at **http://www.cnn. com/STYLE/Index.html**

✥ Fashion Net: The entrance to the fashion industry's pages is at **http://www.triple.com/fashion-net/**

The Fashion Page: **http://www.charm.net/~jakec/**

Internet Horoscopes: **http://www.ws.pipex.com/ tis/horoscop/horo5.htm**

You've Gotta Laugh

Britcomedy Digest: From Benny Hill to the newest alternative comedy, at **http://www.cathouse. org/BritishComedy/BD/**

Comedy Central: **http://www.comcentral.com/ com-menu.html**

Highly Illogical: The deeply yucky music and poetry of Leonard "Spock" Nimoy are at **http:// www.ama.caltech.edu/~mrm/kirk/ spock.html**

The Keeper of Lists: Vote for your favorites, but beware, some of the lists are very silly indeed. **http://www.dtd.com/keepers/**

Netnun: A genuine reverend sister tends to your spiritual needs and cracks some pretty good gags at **http://www.columbia.edu/~jd23/ cybernun.html**

Penn & Teller: **http://www.solinas.com/ penn-n-teller/**

Real Newspaper Headlines: "Iraqi head seeks arms" and funnier examples at **http://pubweb.acns. nwu.edu/~bil874/comedy/occup/news-hea.htm**

TURN THAT NOISE DOWN!
MUSIC

The Internet is hip and happening, so it's no wonder loads of bands are getting their music and videos online. Check these out.

General Music Sites

⬦ Country Music: **http://www.tpoint.net/Users/ wallen/country/country.html**

⬦ Discoweb: **http://www.msci.memphis.edu/ ~ryburnp/discoweb.html**

⬦ Hyperreal: The immense home of all things techno and ambient; drift off to **http:// hyperreal.com/**

⬦ IUMA: Huge, flashy music site with band links galore; strain your modem at **http://www. iuma.com/**

✤ Jammin' Reggae Archives: **http://orpheus.ucsd. edu/jammin/**

Jazzweb: **http://www.nwu.edu/WNUR/jazz/**

✤ Music Base: Very cool home of the new Britpop, at **http://www.musicbase.co.uk/**

Music Network: **http://www.music.network.com/**

✤ Paradox Hip-Hop Links: **http://ubmail.ubalt. edu/~rmills/hiphop.html**

Similarities Engine: Feed in your fave groups and it'll tell you what else you might like. Great fun, at **http://www.webcom.com/~se/**

✤ The Ultimate Band List: **http://american. recordings.com/WWWoM/ubl/ubl.shtml**

Record Companies

Capitol Records: **http://www.hollywoodandvine. com/**

Elektra: **http://www.elektra.com/**

Geffen: **http://www.geffen.com/**

Motown: The home of soul has several sites, but the best is at **http://www.elmail.co.uk/ motown**

Sony: **http:// www.sony. com/**

Sub Pop: **http:// www.subpop. com/**

Virgin: **http:// www.vmg. co.uk/**

Warner Bros: **http://www. wbr.com/**

Netscape: Subpop Wompus Hunt

Netsite: http://www.subpop.com/

S·U·B P·O·P online

"One World, One Network"

86% of 14K (at 87 bytes/sec, 22 se

Bands

Paula Abdul: **http://www2.csn.net/~danzirin/ paula.html**

Aerosmith: **http://coos.dartmouth.edu/~joeh/**

Beastie Boys: **http://www.nando.net:80/music/ gm/BeastieBoys/**

The Beatles: **http://phymat.bham.ac.uk/ RobinsDJ/beatles/index.html**

Beck: **http://mxh160.rh.psu.edu/Docs/Beck. html**

Bon Jovi: **http://www.s-gimb.lj.edus.si/pter/ bj/bj.html**

Mariah Carey: **http://www.wi.leidenuniv.nl/ ~pverheij/mariah.html**

Bob Dylan: **http://www.cis.ohio-state.edu/ hypertext/faq**

Foo Fighters: **http://www.muohio.edu/ ~carmance/foo/index.html**

Grateful Dead: **http://www.cs.cmu.edu/~mleone/ dead.html**

Green Day: **http://www.greenday.com/**

Guns 'n' Roses: **http://www.teleport.com/ ~boerio/gnr-home.html**

Michael Jackson: **http://www.sony.com/ Music/ArtistInfo/MichaelJackson/main. html**

Madonna: **http://www.buffnet.net/~steve772/ maddy.html**

Megadeth: **http://bazaar.com/Megadeth/ Megadeth.html**

Nirvana: **http://seds.lpl.arizona.edu/~smiley/ nirvana/home.html**

Pearl Jam: **http://vinny.csd.mu.edu/cygnus/ vitrev.html**

Portishead: **http://gladstone.uoregon.edu/
    ~jbunik/portishead.html**
Elvis Presley: **http://sunsite.unc.edu/elvis/
    elvishom.html**
Prince: New Power Network: **http://morra.ed.
    tudelft.nl/npn/**
Public Enemy: **http://www.me.tut.fi/~tpaanane/
    pe.html**
Radiohead: **http://www.musicbase.co.uk/
    music/radiohead/**
Rancid: **http://turnpike.net/metro/punk/
    rancid.htm**
REM: **http://www.halcyon.com/rem/index.html**
Rolling Stones: **http://www.stones.com/**
Seal: **http://www.wbr.com/seal1/sealseal.htm**
Smashing Pumpkins: **http://www.ici.net/
    cust_pages/heurichp/PumpkinPatch.html**
Soul Asylum: **http://www.crown.net/~wirtes/
    sa/soulasylum.html**
Soundgarden: **http://www.cerberus.co.uk/
    cdj/readingcarlsbergmm/mm/soundgar.
    html**
U2: **http://www.xs4all.nl/~pj/cm_index.html**
Neil Young: **http://www.bridge.net/~hyperust/**

Magazines and Zines
Addicted to Noise: Superb alternative rock e-zine;
    check out **http://www.addict.com/ATN/**
Ben Is Dead: Just the coolest e-zine ever; cruise by
    **http://140.174.164.2/~johnl/e-zine-list/zines/
    ben-is-dead.html**
Chaos Control: All things industrial pound out from
    http://www.ids.net/~chaos/chaos.html

Foxy: Better than *Sassy*. Much. **http://www. tumyeto.com/tydu/foxy/foxy.htm**

Nadine Magazine: Cute college music mag grooves along at **http://pantheon.cis.yale. edu/~tpole/nadine/home_page.html**

Rolling Stone: **http://rstone.com.au/music/ rstone/**

PLAY THE GAME!
HOBBIES AND GAMES

From Lego to sophisticated fantasy role-playing games, they're all online.

Fun . . .

Barbies Galore: **http://silver.ucs.indiana.edu/ ~jwarf/barbie.html**

Emily's Pog Page: **http://www1.usa1.com/ ~aycruma/pogs.html#index**

Hand Puppet Activity Page: **http://fox.nstn.ca/ ~puppets/activity.html**

Lego: **http://legowww.homepages.com/**

Origami: The best of the paper-folding pages starts at **http://www.cs.ubc.ca/spider/jwu/ origami.html**

Pez: **http://www.cs.ucdavis.edu/~telford/ pez.html**

. . . and Games

Card Games Page: **http://www.cs.man.ac.uk/ card-games**

✧ Complete Role-playing Resource Page: **http:// www.cqs.washington.edu/~surge/rpg.html**

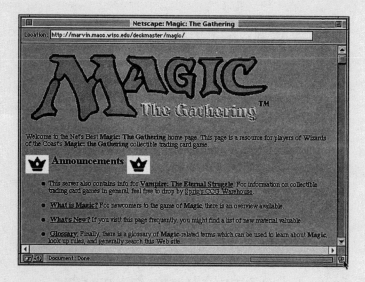

Magic: the Gathering: **http://marvin.macc. wisc.edu/deckmaster/magic/**

Pinball Pasture: **http://www.lysator.liu.se/ pinball/**

Puzzle Depot: **http://iquest.com/~pinnacle/ index.shtml**

WWW Entertainment Package: **http://www. dbai.tuwien.ac.at/cgi-bin/rusch_select/ help/small/**

MORTAL HEDGEHOG TREK MASTER IV COMPUTER GAMES

Links and Demo Sites

DoomGate: **http://doomgate.cs.buffalo. edu/**

Andy Eddy's FAQ Site: You want game cheats?

You got 'em, from **http://brawl.mindlink.
net/pub/vidgames/faqs/**

✦ Gamelink: Ignore the background patterns and this
is a pretty neat selection of PC demos; hop
to **http://ccwf.cc.utexas.edu/~hristos/
gamelink.html**

Game Oasis: Stuck on level nineteen and can't get
any further? Check out the walk-throughs at this
useful site. **http://www.cyberspace.com:
80/acroft/**

✦ Gamers Ledge: Latest reviews of the latest games;
trust the guys at **http://www.medio.net/users/
mgodsey/games/html**

Games & Demos: **http://www.ensta.fr/internet/
dos-windows/games-demos**

✦ The Games Domain: This awesome collection
of demos (including Doom of course), cheats,

and fanzines might be the best games site on
the Net, period. **http://www.gamesdomain.
co.uk/**

◈ Happy Puppy: Weird and wonderful games, plus
links to software houses around the world; all
at **http://happypuppy.com/**

Kev's Videogame Page: Take a look at how
videogames used to be. **http://www.
vdospk.com/home1/kevinp/games/index.
html**

PC Gaming Info: **http://www.peganet.com/
~wcaughey**

◈ Space Weenies Home Page: **http://www.
rubyslippers.com/spaceweenie**

Game Companies

Activision: **http://www.activision.com**

Domark: **http://www.domark.com/domark/**

Electronic Arts: Yet more demos and huge movie clips
to download; hang around at **http://www.
ea.com/**

Lucasarts: **http://www.lucasarts.com**

Maxis: **http://www.maxis.com/maxhome.
html**

Microprose: The flight simulation kings, but a very
graphics heavy site, so bring a book along to
http://www.microprose.com/

Nintendo: **http://www.nintendo.com/**

Origin: Fly those Wings of Glory with the free

downloadable demos from **http://www. ea.com/origin.html**

Playstation Home Page: **http://www.gamezero. com/team0/gmezero/playstationhome**

Sega: **http://www.segaoa.com/**

NERD CENTRAL!
WEIRD STUFF

Some people do new and cool things with the Net. Unfortunately, these do not.

Great Thinkers of Our Time

Charlie's Sneaker Pages: Somebody else with too much spare time, at **http://sneakers.pair. com**

Disaster of the Day: Find out what else went wrong on the day you were born, at **http://www. ora.com:8080/cgi-bin/crash-cal**

Klingon Language Institute: Take an obsession way too far at **http://www.kli.org/klihome.html**

Life at Dave's Apartment: Some dorky students are online. **http://www.csv.warwick.ac.uk/ ~esufl/**

Nerds Revolutionary Front: They're taking over! **http://www.gold.net/users/av78/index. html**

Nerd Test: Are you a geek? Take the quiz at **http://spider.lloyd.com/~dragon/ nerdtest.html**

R. "Bud" Philson: The uncrowned king of the air-guitar rocks out at **http://www.digitalrag. com/mirror/air/air.html**

Net Cameras

Big Sky Cam: The Montana skyline. Not very thrilling. **http://www.gomontana.com/skycam.html**

Car Wash Cam: **http://www.sarabande.com/default.html**

Iguana Cam: **http://iguana.images.com/dupecam.html**

Kitchen Cam: What's everybody eating at Berkeley Systems? **http://www.berksys.com/www/funtour/takepic.html**

The Refreshing Fishcam: **http://www1.netscape.com/fishcam/fish_refresh.html**

See the Live Ants: Yup, it's an ant farm! **http://sec.dgsys.com/AntFarm.html**

Snowball Cam: Aim at someone's head and click, at **http://www.rl.af.mil:8001/Odds-n-Ends/sbcam/rlsbcam.html**

Trivial Pursuits

Ask Mr Puddy: Look, it's a *cat*, it can't help you with your problem. **http://www.sils.umich.edu/~nscherer/AskPuddy.html**

Build a Card: Design a tacky birthday card for someone you don't like at **http://infopages.com/card/**

Carlos' Coloring Book: Are you an artist? Then you won't want to drop in at **http://robot0.ge.uiuc.edu/~carlosp/color/**

Interactive Railroad: Play with the electric train set at **http://rr-vs.informatik.uni-ulm.de/rrbin/ui/RRPage.html**

Mike & Anthony's Wired Room: Turn the fan on.

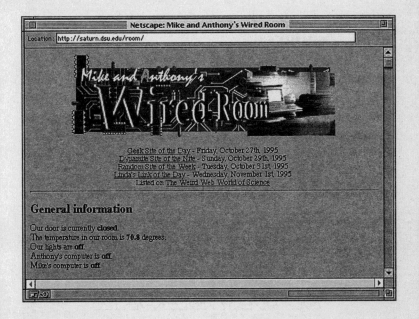

Turn it off again. Go away. **http://saturn.dsu.edu/room/**

Mr. Edible Starchy Tuber Head: Dan Quayle's favorite friend, at **http://winnie.acsu.buffalo.edu/potatoe/**

Online Gardening: Tend the flowers by controlling a robot arm at **http://www.usc.edu/dept/garden/**

Sock Puppet Page: **http://www.unitedmedia.com/comics/dilbert/puppets/**

Strawberry Pop-Tart Flame Thrower: Do not try this at home. **http://cbi.tamucc.edu/~pmichaud/toast/**

URouLette: You'll never know where you end up when you play at **http://www.uroulette.com:8000/**

JOCK ALERT!
SPORTS

Sport fans are way enthusiastic. The Net is crammed to the gills with fans. Put the two together, and . . .

Ball Games

@Bat: The official source for U.S. Major League Baseball information is **http://www2.pcy. mci.net/mlb/index.html**

ESPNet Sportszone: **http://espnet.sportszone.com/**

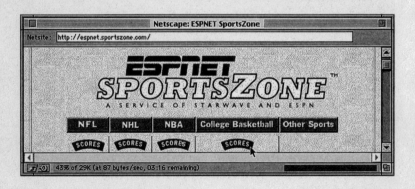

✥ Fastball: You want Major League baseball news right now? You got it at **http://www.fastball. com/**

GNN Basketball: **http://gnn.com/gnn/metal/ sports/basketball/indx.html**

NBC Golf Tour: **http://www.golf.com/**

NFL Football Server: **http://www4.nando.net/ SportServer/football/nfl.html**

Soccer Pages: **http://www.sportsnetwork.com/ soccer/soccer.html**

✧ Tennis Worldwide: **http://www.xmission.com/
~gastown/tennis/**

Ten Pin Bowling Information: **http://www.rpi.
edu/~miller3/bowling.html**

World Wide Ping-pong: **http://www.asahi-net.
or.jp/~Z4MKS/wwpp.html**

✧ World-Wide Web of Sport: **http://www.tns.lcs.
mit.edu/cgibin/sports**

Other Sports

The Boomerang Page: **http://www.dcs.ed.ac.uk/
home/mxm/personal/boom/boomerang.html**

The Boxing Page: **http://lemur.cit.cornell.edu/
boxing/boxing.html**

The Climbing Archive: Advice and maps, equipment
and personal stories from the climbing world;
start your ascent at **http://www.dtek.chalmers.
se/Climbing/index.html**

Gorp Fishing Resources: **http://www.gorp.com:
80/gorp/activity/fishing.htm**

1998 Winter Olympics: At Nagano in Japan they're
already getting ready. **http://www.linc.
or.jp/Nagano/**

Santa Cruz Surfing Museum: **http://www.cruzio.
com/arts/scva/surf.html**

Sports Illustrated for Kids: **http://pathfinder.com/
@@9WlZsVHUowEAQAB7/SIFK/index.html**

Ultimate Frisbee Page: **http://www.cs.
rochester.edu/ulferguson/ultimate/**

White Tiger Kung Fu Kuan: **http://www.halcyon.
com/tomca/wtiger.html**

Windsurfing: **http://wmi.cais.com/www/
windsurf/index.html**

VROOM, VROOM!
TRANSPORTATION

Trains, boats and planes . . . and bicycles, hang-gliders and rollerblades. If you can travel on it, chances are there's a Web site devoted to it.

Airships: **http://spot.colorado.edu/~dziadeck/ zeppelin.html**

✧ Aladdin Sailing Index: **http://www.aladdin.co. uk:80/sihe/**

✧ All Things Automotive: **http://www.webcom. com/~autodir**

Ballooning: **http://sunsite.unc.edu/ballooning/**

How to Ride a Unicycle: **http://nimitz.mcs. kent.edu/~bkonarsk/howtoride.html**

Motorcycle Online: **http://motorcycle.com/ motorcycle.html**

✧ Railroad Internet Resources: **http://www-sce. ucsd.edu/users/bowdidge/railroad/ rail-home.html**

Skateboard.com: **http://skateboard.com/tydu/ skatebrd/skate.htm**

Thrust SSC Server: The land-speed record is up for grabs at **http://thrustssc.digital.co.uk/ thrustssc/html/thrust.htm**

US Navy Submarines: **http://www.cftnet.com/ members/sturgeon/submarin.html**

WHERE IS THAT?
GEOGRAPHY AND TRAVEL

Whether you want to go on vacation or just have homework, the Net is full of information about all the countries of the world.

Travel

Asia Online: Essential travel info for the Pacific rim countries, at **http://silkroute.com**

CIA World Factbook: A fact-packed worldwide guide for spies and civilians alike, at **http://www. odci.gov/**

GNN Travel Resource Center: Travel guides to every country on the planet; take a trip to **http:// www.gnn.com/gnn/gnn/meta/travel/ index.html**

Lonely Planet Tourist Center: Lavish details of just about every destination around the globe from people who've actually been there; set off to **http://www.lonelyplanet.com/**

Rec.Travel Library: The best news, reports and anecdotes from the newsgroup of the same name, at **http://www.nectect.or.th/rec-travel/ index.html**

Timex World Time: Click anywhere on the world map

and it'll tell you the time, at **http://www.
timeinc.com/vibe/vibeworld/worldmap.
html**

Travelmag: A wonderful traveling companion and
guide to the world, at **http://www.travelmag.
co.uk/travelmag**

Can We Go There?

Antarctica: **http://pen1.pen.k12.va.us/~alloyd/
AAA.html**

Arab Emirates: **http://emirates.net.ae/**

Argentina: **http://gopher.ar:70/1/turismo**

Egypt Interactive: **http://www.channel1.com/
users/mansoorm/**

France: **http://www.paris.org/**

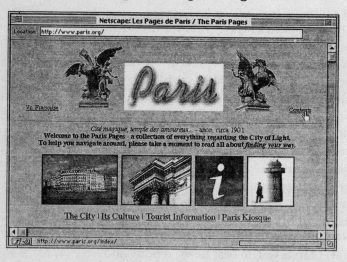

Germany: **http://www.berlin-bear.de/**

Hong Kong: **http://www.hk.super.net/~webzone/
hongkong.html**

Ireland: **http://www.paddynet.ie**

Israel: **http://www1.huji.ac.il/jeru/jerusalem.html**

Japan: Take a tour via **http://w3.cortland.com/ electrazine/japantour/default.html**

or visit the official tourist board site at
http://www.jnto.go.jp/

Tokyo **http://kiku.stanford.edu:80/ LWT/TOKYO/tokyo_home.html**

Pakistan: **http://www.odci.gov/94fact/country/ 185.html**

Russia: **http://www.cs.toronto.edu/~mes/russie/ moscow/main.html**

South Africa: **http://aztec.co.za/biz/africa**

Spain: **http://www.ujl.es/spain_www.html**

Sweden: **http://www.westnet.se/sweden/**

Thailand: **http://www.mahidol.ac.th/ Thailand/Thailand-main.html**

United Kingdom: Use the interactive map of the UK
and Ireland at **http://www.cs.ucl.ac.uk/misc/ uk/intro.html**

Buckingham Palace **http://www. londonmall.co.uk/palace/**

Edinburgh **http://www.efr.hw. ac.uk/EDC/Edinburgh.html**

London **http://www.cs.ucl.ac.uk/misc/ uk/london.html**

USA: The Train Ride Across America is now leaving
from **http://gold.interlog.com/~lavender/ hometra.html**

The Grand Canyon **http://www.kbt. com/gc/**

Hawaii **http://www.satlab.hawaii.edu/ space/hawaii/**

Las Vegas **http://www.infi.net/vegas/ online**

New York **http://mosaic.echonyc.com/
~voice/mighttit.htm**
Yellowstone National Park **http://www.
forestry.umt.edu/yellowstone/**

PARLEZ-VOUS INTERNET?
LANGUAGES

There are resources for many languages, including on-line tutorials and services run for native speakers.

ARTFL Project: Database of the French language; start
at **http://tuna.uchicago.edu/ARTFL.html**
✛ Human Languages: Links to every language on
Earth at **http://www.willamette.edu/
~tjones/Language-Page.html**
Italian: Listen with Professore Antonio at
http://www.eat.com/learn-italian.html
Russian for Travelers: You'll need a Cyrillic typeface
before you try **http://insti.physics.sunysb.edu/
~mmartin/languages/russian/russian.html**
Web Spanish Lessons: ¿No habla Internet? **http://
www.willamette.edu/~tjones/Spanish/
Spanish-main.html**

GREEN STUFF
NATURE/ENVIRONMENT

There are sites devoted to all types of animals, and even more for those who want to help protect them. Get back to nature with these home pages.

The World Around Us
✛ Acme Pet: If you can keep it as a pet it's here.

http://www.acmepet.com/

Bird Web: **http://www.abdn.ac.uk/~nhi019/
intro.html**

✧ Canine Web Links: **http://www.life.uiuc.edu/
physiology/kathy/links.html**

Cat House: **http://cathouse-fcc.org/**

Entomology Image Gallery: **http://www.
public.iastate.edu/~entomology/
ImageGallery.html**

Equinet: **http://horses.product.com/**

Fish Information Service: Or FINS for short!
http://www.actwin.com/fish/index.html

The Hamster Page: **http://www.tela.bc.ca/
hamster.**

Missouri Botanical Garden: **http://www.
mobot.org/**

✧ Netvet/Electronic Zoo: **http://netvet.wustl.
edu/ssi.htm**

Ocean Planet: **http://seawifs.gsfc.nasa.gov/
ocean_planet.html**

Poochnet: **http://www.aescon.com/poochnet/**

Robin's Nest: **http://www.mindspring.com/
~bclark/**

Sheep Home Page: **http://ttsw.com/HenrysSheep/
SheepHomePage.html**

Squashed Bug Zoo: Bzzzzzzzzz . . . splat! Check the
aftermath at **http://albert.ccae.virginia.edu/
~dcm3c/zoo.html**

Turtle Trax: **http://www.io.org/~bunrab/**

Wolves on the Web: **http://wwwnncc.scs.unr.
edu/wolves/desertm.html**

Zoonet Image Archives: Animal pictures, they got
'em! **http://www.mindspring.com/
~zoonet/gallery.html**

Save the World!

Earth Island: Save a sea turtle or protect a forest, starting at **http://www.earthisland.org/ei/**

✦ EcoNet: A world of environmental home pages, links, and more; look at **http://www.econet. apc.org/econet/**

✦ Environmental Resources Information Network: Another great place to start your campaign is at **http://kaos.erin.gov.au/erin.html**

Greenpeace: Very well-run headquarters of the scourge of polluters and whalers; start at **http://www.greenpeace.org/**

National Wildlife Federation: **http://www.nwf. org/nwf/home.html**

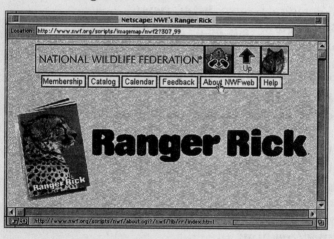

SAFETY GOGGLES MUST BE WORN!
SCIENCE

Scientists have always loved computers and the Internet, which was originally set up to carry their data. Now you can access these sites, too.

Biology

Digital Anatomist Program: Astonishing computer images of every part of the human body; poke around at **http://www1.biostr.washington. edu/DigitalAnatomist.html**

Interactive Frog Dissection: Oh, gross! Still, beats doing it to a real one. **http://george.ibl.gov/ ITG.hm.pg.docs/dissect/dissect.html**

The Interactive Patient: Fact-packed resource for students of medicine and human biology as a whole; say "aaaah" at **http://medicus. marshall.edu/medicus.html**

The Earth

CTI Center for Geology, Geography & Meteorology: **http://www.geog.le.ac.uk/cti/index.html**

Earth's Active Volcanoes: **http://www.geo.mtu. edu/volcanoes/world.html**

Gateway to the Antarctic: **http://icair.iac.org.nz/**

Seismosurfing: **http://www.geophysics. washington.edu/seismosurfing.html**

Volcano World: **http://volcano.und.nodak.edu/**

World Population: Find out how many of us there are right this second, at **http://sunsite.unc.edu/ lunar/popanim.html**

Outer Space

Asteroid & Comet Impact Hazard: Where will the next one hit? **http://ccf.arc.nasa.gov/sst/**

Astronomy Café: **http://www2.ari.net/home/ odenwald/afe.html**

Declassified Satellite Photos: Fresh from the confidential U.S. government files: **http:// edcwww.cr.usgs.gov/dclass/dclass.html**

Galileo: The mission to Jupiter continues at
http://www.jpl.nasa.gov/galileo
NASA: From the first manned missions to the current
Shuttle tests. **http://www.gsfc.nasa.gov/**

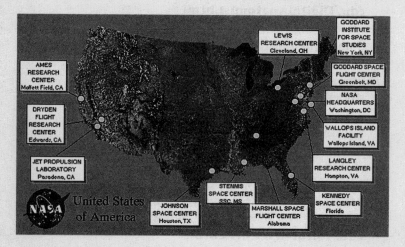

The Nine Planets: An awesome interactive trip
through the Solar System. **http://seds.lpl.
arizona.edu/billa/tnp/nineplanets.html**
UFO Directory: **http://galaxy.einet.net/
galaxy/Community/Parascience/
Unidentified-Flying-Objects/**

Pure Science
Ask Dr. Neutrino: Any question you want (about
physics) at **http://nike.phy.bris.ac.uk/dr/
ask.html**
It's New!: Technological innovations or useless
gadgets? You decide at **http://www.cts.com/
~itsnew/**

✧ Math Internet Links: Get help with your math at **http://www.gnn.com/gnn/meta/edu/curr/ math/res/links/index.html**

Understanding Our Planet Through Chemistry: **http://helios.cr.usgs.gov/gips/aii-in14.htm**

STUFF YOUR FACE!
FOOD AND DRINK

You don't need to watch French chefs on TV to decide what to cook for dinner. Just check out these tasty Web sites instead.

Product Placement

Ben & Jerry's: **http://www.benjerry.com**

Breakfast Cereal Hall of Fame: Hey, anyone remember Quisp? **http://198.3.11.222/index.html**

CheeseNet: The history of cheese. Cheese making. Cheese varieties. Cheese. Cheese. Cheese. **http://www.efn.org/~kpw/cheesenet96/**

Coca-Cola Corporation: **http://www.cocacola. com**

eGG: The Electronic Gourmet Guide has stories from the food world. **http://www.2way.com:80/ food/egg/index.html**

✧ The Food Resource: Links to assorted food sites, and masses of pictures of, well, food; eat it up at **http://www.orst.edu/food-resource/food.html**

Frito-Lay: **http://www.fritolay.com/**

Kellogg Clubhouse: **http://www.kelloggs.com/**

Mama's Cucina: Ragu spaghetti sauce site with recipes that, strangely, all seem to need a certain ingredient. Drop in at **http://www.eat.com/**

Official Snapple Home Page: **http://www.snapple.com/**

Pepsi Cola: **http://www.pepsi.co.uk**

Pizza Hut: **http://www.pizzahut.com**

Tasty Recipes

The Burrito Page: Tasty Tex-Mex tidbits at **http://www.infobahn.com/pages/rito.html**

Cajun Family Recipe Book: **http://www.net-connect.net/cajun/home-c.htm**

Chili Recipes: **http://www.tpoint.net/~wallen/chili.html**

Chocolate Recipes: **http://www.godiva.com/recipes/chocolatier/index.html**

Amy Gale Recipe Index: **http://www.vuw.ac.nz/who/Amy.Gale/recipes/**

Indonesian Food & Recipes: **http://bromo.parokinet.org/docs/recipe.html**

Ridiculously Easy Recipes: **http://www.sar.usf.edu/~zazuetaa/recipe.html**

Stuart's Chinese Recipes: **http://www-hons-cs.dcs.st-andrews.ac.uk/~sab/Chinese_Recipes.html**

Tasty Insect Recipes: "Tasty" is probably pushing

it, unless you really enjoy the thought of eating grasshoppers and bugs. **http://www.public. iastate.edu/~entomology/InsectsAsFood. html**

The Virtual Recipe Book: But hey, use real food, okay? **http://www.pathfinder.com/ KeFZ40BjAAIAQOgX/cgi-bin/twep/ recipe.cgi**

NEWS AT ELEVEN
NEWS

Net-based news is updated as it happens, with services across the globe giving their own viewpoint on current events.

News

CNN Interactive: News updated every hour, 24 hours a day; ten sections including Sport, Showbiz, Style, Business, etc. **http://www.cnn.com/**

New York TimesFax: Short and snappy news items from **http://nytimesfax.com/**

The Press Association: All the news from London at
http://www.pa.press.net/
United Nations News: **http://nearnet.gnn.com/
gnn/meta/travel/res/newsgath.html**

World Newspapers
Asahi Shimbun: Japanese daily, from **http://www.
asahi.com/english/english.html**
Bermuda Sun: Caribbean weekly **http://www.
bermudasun.org/news**
Cambodia Times: Cambodian weekly **http://
www.jaring.my/at-asia/camb_at_asia/
cambodia/html**
China News Digest: **http://www.cnd.org/**
Gazeta Online: Polish daily at **http://info.fuw.edu.
pl/gw/0/gazeta.html**
The Hindu: Indian national paper at **http://www.
webpage.com/hindu/**
Irish Times on the Web: **http://www.irish-
times.ie**
Jerusalem Post: Famous Israeli paper is at **http://
www.jpost.co.il/**
The Post: Zambia's first Web newspaper is at **http://
www.zamnet.zm**
San Jose Mercury News: California daily at **http://
www.sjmercury.com/**
Scottish Daily Record/Sunday Mail: **http://
www.record-mail.co.uk/rm/drsm/front1.
html**
USA Today: **http://www.usatoday.com/web1.htm**
Village Voice: What's hip and happening in NYC,
from **http://www.dc.enews.com/
magazines/village/**

Wall Street Journal: **http://www.wsj.com/cgi-bin/
index.cgi**

RED SKY AT NIGHT
WEATHER

The weather? That's pretty dull, right? Think again and
take a look at these sites. Here are up-to-the-minute
satellite photos and real-time space shots of distant
parts of the globe.

Climate Diagnostics Center: Everything you ever
wanted to know about the Earth's climate.
http://www.cdc.noaa.gov/
Current Weather Maps: Up-to-the-minute forecasts
for your area are at **http://wxweb.msu.edu/
weather**
Hurricane Watch: **http://www.netcreations.com/
hurricane/**
National Severe Storms Laboratory: **http://www.
nssl.uoknor.edu/**
Northern Lights: **http://www.uit.no/npt/
homepage-npt.en.html**
Weather in Tromso: Guess it's handy if you live in
Tromso, at **http://www.cs.uit.no/~ken/
images/big/weather.gif**

TAKE ME TO YOUR LEADER
GOVERNMENT AND POLITICS

The Government and the Law
CIA Factbook: **http://www.odci/gov/cia/
publications/**

Congress E-Mail List: **http://www.webcom.com/ ~leavitt/cong.html**

FBI: See who's on the FBI's Ten Most Wanted list at **http://www.fbi.gov/toplist.htm**

The Flag of the U.S.A.: **http://www.elkgrove.k12. il.us/usflag/usflag.html**

NYPD: **http://www.cyi.nyc.ny.us/nyclink/ html/nypd/finest.html**

The Pentagon: **http://www.dtic.dla.mil/ defenselink/pubs/pentagon**

Road to the White House: **http://www.ipt.com/ vote/**

The State Department: **http://dosfan.lib.uic.edu/ dosfan.html**

U.S. Senate: **http://www.senate.gov/**

The White House: Take the all-new tour of the Oval

Office with Socks as your guide from **http://www.whitehouse.gov/White_House/html/White_House_Home.html**

International Organizations
Amnesty International: **http://organic.com/Non.profits/Amnesty/**
International Red Cross: **http://www.ifrc.org/**

BLESS YOU!
RELIGION

Whatever faith you follow, you will find sites devoted to all aspects of world religions on the Internet.

The Bible Gateway: **http://www.calvin.edu/cgi-bin/bible**

Welcome to the Bible Gateway

✧ Catholic Resources: **http://www.cs.cmu.edu:8001/Web/People/spok/catholic.html**

⟡ Facets of Religion: **http://marvin.biologie. uni-freiburg.de/%7Eamueller/religion/**

⟡ Global Hindu Electronic Network: **http:// rbhatnagar.csm.uc.edu:8080/hindu_ universe.html**

⟡ Hare Krishna Home Page: **http://www.webcom. com/~ara/**

⟡ Islamic Resources MetaPage: **http://wings. buffalo.edu.student-life/sa/muslim/is/ isl.html**

⟡ Journal of Buddhist Ethics: **http://www.psu.edu/ jbe/present.html**

⟡ Judaism & Jewish Resources: **http://shamash. nysernet.org/trb/judaism.html**

⟡ Religious Studies Resources: A great place to start exploring the world's religions, at **http://www. dur.ac.uk/"dth3maf/gresham.html**

THE HALL OF SHAME AN INTERNET NIGHTMARE!

We saved these until last, because, well, you probably wouldn't have believed us if we had told you this stuff earlier. These are where the *real* wackos hang out!

Stupid

Adopt-a-Dogz: Download a doggie to your hard drive, if you must, from **http://www.pfmagic.com/ dogz/adopt/**

Drop Squad: A deep and meaningful scientific study of what happens when different objects are dropped down stairwells. **http://www. dropsquad.com**

Fashion for Dogs: Man's best friend gets a wardrobe makeover at **http://carpi1.shiny.it/fashiond/fashiond.htm**

House of Lost Socks: Oh, there it is! Start the search at **http://www.caprica.com/~jmares/house_of_socks.html**

Talk to My Cat: It's a picture of a cat. Say something. **http://queer.clip.cs.cmu.edu/cgi-bin/talktocat**

What Miles Is Watching: There's nothing we'd rather do than find out what Miles has on his TV in California. Just let us call up **http://www.csua.berkeley.edu/~milesm/ontv.html**

What's in My Desk Drawer: Don't you understand? We don't care! **http://www.crayola.cse.psu.edu/~goodman/desk.html**

Just Plain Bad

A-baa: It's a sheep. Click. Baaa. Leave. **http://www.obsolete.com/baa/audio/baa.aiff**

Blue Dog Can Count: Give her a math problem, she'll bark the answer. Ruff. **http://hp8.ini.cmu.edu:5550/bdf.html**

⟡ Buttons Galore: And you thought the Really Big Red Button was lame . . . **http://www.sas.upenn.edu/~pitharat/buttons.html**

Foam Bath Fish Time: Some fish-shaped bath sponges. Dumb. **http://redwood.northcoast.com/cgi-bin/fishtime?-5**

Light Up the World: The world is in shadow. Click to light it up. Or don't. **http://scifi.emi.net/cgi-bin/light-cgi/**

Marshmallow Peep Page: Birds made of
   marshmallows. Happy Easter! **http://www.
   wam.umd.edu/~ejack/peep.html**

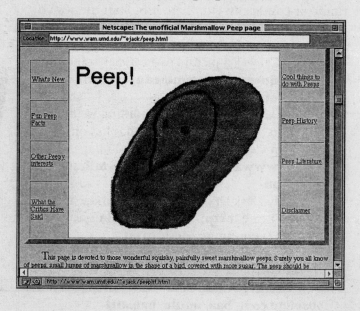

Mind Reader: Click on the man's picture and he'll tell
   you what you're thinking, at **http://nlu.nl.edu/
   ben/mind/**

Online Lava Lamp: Ooh, it's the 1960s! **http://
   ascott.com/hal/htmls/lava.html**

Ranjit's Lunch: What's Ranjit Bhatnager having for
   lunch? Who cares? **http://oz.sas.upenn.edu/
   miscellany/lunch.html**

The Really Big Red Button Which Doesn't Do
   Anything: It's big, it's red, and nothing happens
   when you press it. **http://www.wam.umd.edu/
   ~twoflowr/button.htm**

Snort, Snort: A stupid sound effect for that special occasion can be downloaded at **http://www.redstar.com/~chris/snort.html**

Todd & Lynne's Photo Album: Oh get a life, will you? **http://www.vvm.com/~tscot/test.html/**

GLOSSARY

These are the most common, but if you come across some really technical phrase you don't know, look it up in the enormous online glossary at **http://www. matisse.net/files/glossary.html**

Access Provider: A company that sells Internet connections.

Anonymous FTP: Way of picking up free software from a data bank.

Archie: A special program that searches for FTP files across an archive.

ASCII: American Standard Code for Information Interchange, also known as "plaintext."

Attachment: A file joined to an e-mail message and sent along with it.

Bandwidth: The maximum amount of information that can be sent through a connection.

Baud Rate: Speed at which a modem sends data, in bps (bits per second).

BBS: Bulletin Board System; a basic system, where you dial in to leave or read messages or files.

Bcc: Blind Carbon Copy; sends an e-mail to another person but conceals the identity of the other recipients.

Bookmark: A file used by a Web browser like Netscape to store the addresses of favorite locations.

Bounced mail: E-mail that didn't get through and was returned to the sender.

Browser: Program used to surf the World Wide Web.

Cc: Carbon Copy; sends a duplicate e-mail to another person.

Channel: A "room" on IRC where you can chat with other people.

Cross-posting: Sending the same message to two or more newsgroups; try not to.

Cyberspace: The virtual world of the Internet.

Dial-up: Regular Internet access you get by ringing up a service provider with your modem.

Digest: A collection of all the messages from a mailing list, sent out as one file every day.

Domain: Each part of your e-mail address is a domain, a specific area of the Net just like a town or street.

Download: To transfer a file from one computer to another.

E-mail: Method of sending letters and other files from one computer to another.

E-zine: Like a magazine—but on the Internet!

FAQ: Frequently Asked Questions; a file of the most common questions and their answers, found in newsgroups and on some Web pages.

Firewall: A program that bars access to certain parts of the Net.

Flame: Angry e-mail reply to something stupid.

FTP: File Transfer Protocol; a way of getting software or other files from a data bank.

Gopher: Nifty but old-fashioned program for searching out and reading Internet files.

Home Page: A person or company's Web pages (or the first page of a larger site).

Host: The computer your modem contacts to get online.

HTML: HyperText Mark-Up Language; computer language used to create World Wide Web sites.

HTTP: HyperText Transfer Protocol; system used to allow you to surf between Web pages.

Internet: Vast interconnected network of computers; often shortened to Net.

IRC: Internet Relay Chat; two-way conversations between people, using a system like e-mail.

ISDN: Professional, high-quality connections; better than regular telephone lines.

ISP: Internet Service Provider; an access provider that gives you all the Internet services.

Listserv: An automatic mailing list handler; an alternative name for a mailing list.

Log off: Disconnecting from your service provider.

Log on: Connecting through your service provider and going online.

Lurking: Reading a newsgroup without posting to it.

Mailing List: A series of e-mails discussing a specific subject that's sent out automatically to your address.

Majordomo: Another automatic mailing list handler.

Mirror: Some FTP and Web sites are so busy that their entire contents are copied to another address to ease the traffic.

Modem: Box of circuits (a "modulator/demodulator") that connects your computer to the telephone line.

Moderated: A channel or newsgroup which is supervised.

Newbie: A newcomer to the Net, or to a specific place such as a newsgroup.

Newsgroup: Discussion group; everyone looking in gets to read comments and reply to them.

Newsreader: Program that lets you access a newsgroup.

Node: Any device connected to the network.

Online: Connected to the Internet.

OSP: Online Service Provider, one of the older BBS-derived access providers that originally didn't offer full Internet access.

PC: Personal Computer.

POP: Point of Presence; place where your telephone line joins that of the company giving you Internet access.

Post: To add your own comments or questions to a newsgroup.

PPP: Point to Point Protocol; the language newer modems use to connect to the Net.

Protocol: The way two different Internet devices talk to each other.

RFC: Request for comments, usually about a program that's not quite finished.

Robot (or Bot): An interactive device such as a search engine that you can send off to find or get something for you.

Server: Computer at your POP that allows you Internet access.

Service Provider: Particular company that handles your Internet access.

Signature File (or .sig): Message or picture, often meant to be funny, that you add to the end of all your e-mail or newsgroup messages; usually made up of letters and punctuation.

SLIP: Serial Line Internet Protocol; the earlier version of PPP which is slowly being replaced.

Smiley: Cute little symbol made of punctuation marks that is meant to express a complex concept or emotion :-); also known as an Emoticon.

Snail mail: The traditional postal service.

Spam: To post the same message to loads of different newsgroups; frowned upon.

Surfing: Moving about the Internet using click-on links.

TCP/IP: Transmission Control Protocol/Internet Protocol; the computer language that your computer uses to talk to your modem and the Net.

Telnet: Precursor to the World Wide Web, a means of accessing data on a distant computer.

Thread: One discussion topic that runs through a newsgroup.

TLA: Three Letter Acronym; a short version of a longer term used to save on typing.

Unix: Computer operating system that most of the Internet is ultimately based on.

URL: Uniform Resource Locator, a World Wide Web address as used by your browser to find a site.

USENET: All the various Newsgroups.

V Series: Various types and speeds of modems, e.g. V32, V34, etc.

WWW: World Wide Web; an interconnected network of files, usually in the form of graphic pages, that makes up most of the Internet; a wonderful place to explore!

WRITE US

If you have any questions or comments, or just want to say Hi, you can e-mail Marc Gascoigne at **marco@ overload.demon.co.uk** He can't promise to reply to every message, but he'd love to hear what you think of this book.

Please note: if you have any real serious technical questions, such as modifying TCP/IP for SLIP connection protocols, or Gophering Telnet through IRC, you should ask your Internet service provider's support desk.

Keep an eye on Penguin Books' home pages for fast-breaking information from the world's best book publisher. Point your Web browser at **http://www. penguin.com**

LOG OFF

It's a tradition with a book like this to end with a reminder of just how amazing the Internet is. But we figure you've gotten the message by now!

The Internet's getting bigger and even better by the second, and it's awesome when you're out there exploring.

Remember your netiquette. See you on the surf.

INDEX